FARRELL MIDDLETON

PERFORMER ENVIRONMENT

A Roadmap to Enhance Your
Performance and Upgrade
Your Environment

FREILING AGENCY

Copyright © 2025 by Farrell Middleton
First Paperback and Hardback Editions

All rights reserved. No part of this publication may be reproduced, distributed, or transmitted in any form or by any means, including photocopying, recording, or other electronic or mechanical methods, without the prior written permission of the publisher, except in the case of brief quotations embodied in critical reviews and certain other noncommercial uses permitted by copyright law. For permission requests, write to the publisher, addressed "Attention: Permissions Coordinator," at the address below.

Some names, businesses, places, events, locales, incidents, and identifying details inside this book have been changed to protect the privacy of individuals.

Published by Freiling Agency, LLC.

P.O. Box 1264
Warrenton, VA 20188

www.FreilingAgency.com

PB ISBN: 978-1-963701-33-3
HB ISBN: 978-1-963701-34-0
E-book ISBN: 978-1-963701-35-7

For my wife Kathy, and my daughters,
Pfeiffer and Collier.

Their incredible positive influences on
my life have made me the person that I am,
and I am forever grateful.

CONTENTS

Preface vii
The Concept xiii

Part 1
A Performer

Introduction to "A Performer" 3
1   The Power of Attitude 9
2   Developing a Wake-up Frame of Mind 17
3   Achieving a High Level of Self-Esteem 23
4   Developing and Maintaining Healthy
        Relationships 31
5   Mastering Communication for Personal and
        Professional Success 39
6   Start the Day Consistently and Stay Engaged 45
7   Strong Work Ethic Produces Good Results 51
8   Be a Problem Solver 57
9   Identify and Develop Skill Sets 65
10   Take on Additional Tasks 71
11   Education and Experience, the Foundation for
        Lifelong Success 79

A Performer Evaluation 86

Part 2
A Environment

Introduction to Environment 91
12   Vision – Defining Purpose and Direction 97

13	Leadership – The Cornerstone of an A Environment	105
14	Structure – Building the Framework for Success	113
15	Commitment: Foundation of Success	121
16	Discipline: The Backbone of Excellence	129
17	Communication: The Lifeline of an A Environment	137
18	Developing and Maintaining Healthy Professional Relationships	147
19	Productivity Drives Success	155
20	Problem-Solving Opportunities	163
21	Great Customer Service Starts from the Inside	173
22	Maximizing Impact by Mastering Your Four Key Resources	183
23	Influence on External Partners	193

A Environment Evaluation 200

Conclusion 203

About the Author 205

PREFACE

What is the most critical factor that shapes your happiness and success? Your attitude.

What is the one resource that every one of us has in equal measure, regardless of our background or circumstances? Your time.

No matter your goal—your destination—the real key to success lies in the journey—your journey.

A POSITIVE ATTITUDE AND TIME SPENT EFFECTIVELY WILL DRIVE THE SUCCESS OF YOUR JOURNEY.

Success in life both personally and professionally, often hinges on the simplest yet most profound actions: taking things one day at a time, nurturing healthy relationships, communicating clearly with those around you, and making the most of every situation. These foundational habits are central to The Bell Curve of Life, my teaching, coaching, and mentoring program, which this book was born out of.

I consult with leaders and share the Bell Curve of Life principles with them. It isn't built on theoretical concepts or fleeting trends—it's grounded in real-life circumstances and the timeless principles people face daily. At its heart lies the "20/60/20" principle. In any group, 20% of individuals are high performers, 60% make up the middle, and the remaining 20% struggle with lower levels of behavior, skills, performance, and results. The program aims to help people move upward—toward the top of the curve—by developing better attitudes, enhancing interpersonal communication, and building stronger relationships. At the professional level, it partners with leaders and teams to create healthier work environments, improve customer service, and foster team dynamics.

Applying the Principles to Life and Work

The Bell Curve of Life works on two levels. Individually, it helps people sharpen their problem-solving skills, improve communication, and adopt a growth mindset. Professionally, it supports organizations by tailoring strategies to specific challenges, boosting employee engagement, and improving internal and external customer service. By focusing on positive attitudes, effective time management, and better collaboration, the program creates a ripple effect that enhances productivity and strengthens relationships across the board.

The materials in this program are timeless. Whether you pick them up today or revisit them in five, ten, or twenty years, the lessons remain relevant. But timeless principles only work if they're applied with intentionality. Success requires approaching the material with an open mind and a commitment to change. As you move through these pages, reflect on how each topic relates to your circumstances. Ask yourself: Where can I make the most significant impact? What changes will create the most value for myself and others? Let this book serve as both a guide and a catalyst for long-term personal and professional growth.

Focus on What Matters Most

Growth begins by identifying your priorities. Life doesn't come with unlimited time or energy, so it's essential to focus on the areas where you can move the needle the most. Ask yourself, "Where am I already excelling, and where do I need improvement?" Too often, we overlook the areas where we're doing well. Take a moment to acknowledge your strengths, then shift your attention to areas that still need development.

This isn't about busywork or solving problems that don't exist. Your time is far too valuable for that. Instead, focus your energy on actions that lead to meaningful progress. Whether improving relationships, enhancing your environment, or tackling professional challenges, choose the things that will leave a lasting impact.

Long-Term Growth, Not Quick Fixes

The Bell Curve of Life isn't about temporary fixes or a "New Year's Resolution" mentality. Too often, people set lofty goals for January 1st, only to abandon them a few days or weeks later. Real change doesn't come from a date on a calendar; it comes from daily commitment and purposeful action.

If you're seeking quick resolutions or short-term motivation, this book might not be for you. But if you're ready to make meaningful, long-lasting improvements, you're in the right place. This book isn't about instant gratification—it's about providing you with the tools and insights to transform your life over the long haul.

The Journey Ahead

Finally, each of the topics in this book could be expanded to be their own book. For example, how many books have been published that relate to positive attitudes and effective leadership?

There are many. If there are other areas that you want to explore, please pursue them to get a deeper perspective. My purpose is to provide a thorough outline for your personal and professional performance improvement, and for your professional environment improvement.

Work on the areas that need work, and that can include finding different material from other authors that go into much greater details on those topics.

That being said, the ideas in this book can be read in just a few hours, but their impact can last a lifetime. Success comes from adopting the right mindset, taking action, and consistently applying learning. Use these principles to elevate your personal and professional life. If you're ready to embrace lasting growth and meaningful change, let's begin this journey together!

THE CONCEPT

Relative to our historical educational grading scale of A, B, C, D, F -

If you put a C Performer in an A Environment, they can become an A Performer

If you put an A Performer in a C Environment, they will become a C Performer and will probably leave.

If business or organizational leaders want to attain A Performance, they must create an A Environment

If you create an A Environment and attain A Performance, success will follow, and failure will be rare.

PART 1

A PERFORMER

INTRODUCTION TO "A PERFORMER"

A "C" performer can absolutely grow into a "B" performer, and a "B" performer has the potential to elevate themselves to an "A" performer. Even those already performing at the top of their game—A performers—can become a better version of themselves. Growth is always possible, as none of us can excel at everything, but we can all improve where it matters most.

Life is a series of choices, and these choices determine how we spend our time and energy. Whether personal or professional, these decisions shape every aspect of our lives—our families, faith, relationships, careers, and even leisure activities. The key to success lies in being intentional about those choices and ensuring they align with our values and goals.

Personal Choices That Shape Us

On a personal level, some people choose to live independently, while others build their lives with a spouse or partner. Some embrace parenthood, whether biologically, through adoption, or within blended families. Whatever path you choose, the goal is to live fully and contentedly within that choice.

Like many aspects of life, faith is deeply personal. While this book won't explore the subject in depth, it's important to recognize that faith can be a powerful influence, offering guidance and strength. Each person's journey in this area is unique and deserves respect.

Relationships also play a critical role in shaping who we are. Some individuals thrive in a close-knit circle of friends, while others prefer a wider network or solitude. Whether introverted, extroverted or somewhere in between, the key is to embrace your natural tendencies while remaining open to change as life evolves.

Career Paths and Professional Growth

Professionally, our journeys are as diverse as we are. Some commit to a single career for a lifetime, particularly in specialized fields like law, medicine, or aviation. Others explore multiple career paths or step in and out of the workforce as life demands. Some dedicate their energy to managing their households, ensuring life runs smoothly for those around them.

Social engagement also enriches our lives. Participating in volunteer organizations, committees, or small groups—such as book clubs or hobby groups—creates personal growth and connection opportunities. These interactions often provide a sense of purpose and fulfillment outside of work and family life.

INTRODUCTION TO "A PERFORMER"

Recreational activities are another key component of a balanced life. Whether you're passionate about lifelong pursuits like golf, tennis, or running or enjoy more physically demanding activities like basketball or soccer, staying active is vital for overall health and well-being. The focus should always be on movement and connection, even as your abilities change with time.

The Foundations of a Performer

The foundations of success—healthy relationships, meaningful interactions, committed effort, and a focus on results—are essential in all aspects of life. Whether personal or professional, these elements are the threads that weave together a life of fulfillment. Growth requires us to invest time and energy in the most critical areas.

The "A performer" is someone who embodies these qualities. They maintain a positive attitude, nurture healthy relationships, communicate effectively, and consistently deliver solid results. While they, like everyone else, face challenges and setbacks, their commitment to excellence ensures steady progress. Their peaks and valleys are less extreme, and their resilience sets them apart.

Levels of Performance

Even A performers—those already excelling—can push themselves further. Professional athletes are a perfect example. A basketball player aiming for more than an 85% free-throw rate, a football kicker striving to increase their success percentage, or a baseball pitcher working to improve their strike rate exemplify the pursuit of excellence. Similarly, performers in any field can identify areas of strength and challenge themselves to grow even more.

B performers have a mix of strengths and areas that need improvement. Their results tend to fluctuate—sometimes delivering strong outcomes, others falling short. Small, focused changes in attitude, effort, or relationships can lead to significant improvements, moving them closer to A-level performance.

C performers often face challenges with attitude, productivity, communication, teamwork, and relationships, resulting in average or inconsistent outcomes. However, this is precisely where the greatest potential for transformation lies. By making small, deliberate improvements, C performers can steadily progress to B-level performance and beyond.

The Journey of Growth

Growth starts with a choice. Are you content with where you are, or do you want to aim higher? You can elevate your performance in any area by focusing on activities that align with a healthy mindset and producing impactful results through intentional effort.

The journey toward improvement often requires guidance from others—family, friends, or professional colleagues. An accountability partner can support and help you stay on track, much like in an exercise program. It's a proven strategy for achieving lasting progress.

Start with the area that will create the biggest positive impact for you and those around you. Once you've progressed in one area, move on to the next.

A steady, intentional process will help you achieve lasting growth and transformation. Whether you aim to move from C to B or B to A, the choice is yours. Growth is always possible—and it starts with taking that first step.

The Bottom Line

Ultimately, every individual has the power to choose their direction. Growth begins with identifying areas of focus and taking that first step toward meaningful improvement. Whether seeking guidance from others, leveraging accountability partners, or consistently evaluating your progress, the path to success is clear: invest where it matters most and let the results speak for themselves.

As you explore the chapters ahead, reflect on the areas of your life—personal and professional—where growth will have the greatest impact. Start small, build momentum, and continue the journey toward becoming the best version of yourself.

A Performer Evaluation

An evaluation survey at the end of this book section will help you assess where you currently stand as an A, B, or C Performer. This will help you identify areas of growth and enhancement. Review this Evaluation Form and conduct a self-rating as you reach each chapter. Try to be honest with yourself. After all of the topics inside this book have been evaluated, pick one or two to focus on for the most impactful improvement. Don't attempt to take on too much at one time. Once noticeable progress has been made, move on to the next one, two, and so on until all topics have been addressed and you've achieved A Performer status in all categories.

1

THE POWER OF ATTITUDE

What is the single most potent factor influencing your success and happiness? It's your attitude. While others and external circumstances may influence it, they can never control it. You have the ultimate say. A positive attitude practiced consistently allows you to navigate life's challenges and opportunities with resilience and grace. The true test of a positive mindset comes when circumstances are less than ideal. It's easy to maintain a good attitude when everything is going well, but the real strength of a positive mindset shines in the face of adversity—whether personal or professional.

A positive attitude creates a ripple effect. It impacts your long-term success, influences those around you, and fosters a constructive environment. It's contagious. Imagine inspiring your team, family, or community with your positive outlook. The possibilities for growth and success are endless when your attitude sets the tone.

Conversely, a negative attitude also spreads quickly. It not only affects your own performance but can demotivate others, creating a toxic environment. Relationships falter, productivity declines and opportunities are missed. Choosing a positive attitude transforms not only your life but the lives of those around you.

Attitude can influence many factors in your life, including:

- **Mental and Physical Health**
  A positive attitude can directly influence your health by creating a positive mindset and reducing stress. A negative attitude will cause anxiety, high stress, and possible depression.
- **Happiness**
  A positive attitude will lead to greater overall satisfaction and higher levels of joy. A negative attitude will lead to feelings of sadness and an overall poor outlook.
- **Relationships**
  A positive attitude will improve communication and can enhance social connections. A negative attitude can strain relationships and will lead to conflict and isolation.
- **Improved self-esteem**
  A positive attitude will lead to higher levels of self-esteem, which can include self-compassion, setting realistic goals, and focusing on personal strengths. A negative attitude can tear down self-esteem through not accepting faults, not achieving goals, and focusing on weaknesses.

- **Enhanced adaptability**
  A positive attitude opens the mind to healthy change and doing things better. A negative attitude will foster a closed mind that will not accept new concepts and ideas, leading to stagnation.

A Story of Positivity: Haven House at Midtown

In 1990/1991, my wife Kathy, our friends Metta and Clyde Johnson, and I opened Haven House at Midtown, Inc., the first hospice for AIDS patients in the Southeastern United States. At the height of the AIDS crisis, this was a monumental and challenging task. Our vision was to create a safe, compassionate facility where patients could receive care during their final days.

We faced numerous obstacles:

- **Regulations:** Securing a Certificate of Need from the Georgia Department of Human Resources was a significant hurdle.
- **Facilities:** We renovated a 90-year-old Midtown Atlanta home into a mini-hospital, tackling ambiguous building codes along the way.
- **Community Pushback:** Neighbors resisted having the facility nearby.

- **Insurance Challenges:** Coverage for AIDS-related care was complex and required significant negotiation.
- **Outreach:** Raising awareness within the healthcare community about our services was a constant challenge.

Despite these difficulties, we maintained a positive attitude. In December 1991, we opened the facility, and two years later, we expanded with another facility next door. Our positivity and resilience made this possible, allowing us to serve patients and their families during their most difficult times.

The Key to Improvement

The journey to improved performance begins with attitude. Whether striving to move from C to B or B to A, your mindset will propel you forward. Small but intentional changes make a significant difference, and by taking charge, you're already on the growth plan. So ask yourself: What kind of impact do you want your attitude to have? Are you ready to shift toward better performance and greater success? The first step is choosing positivity.

The A Performer: Optimistic Achievers

A performers consistently maintain a positive attitude, even in challenging situations. This resilience is a defining characteristic. They see difficulties not as obstacles but as opportunities to sharpen their skills and strengthen their performance. External circumstances and others may influence their attitude, but they never allow it to be controlled by anyone but themselves. This mindset enables A performers to excel consistently in their relationships, productivity, and results.

For A performers, challenges are an opportunity to grow. Just as athletes push their limits to stay in peak condition, A performers embrace adversity to maintain their edge. They thrive under pressure and consistently set themselves apart by rising to meet difficulties with optimism and determination.

The B Performer: Inconsistent Contributors

B performers demonstrate fluctuating attitudes. On good days, when everything runs smoothly, they exhibit positivity and productivity. But when faced with challenges, their mindset often dips, and their outlook turns negative. They may recover over time, but the inconsistency limits their overall effectiveness.

Tips to Become an A Performer:

- Remember, your attitude is yours to control. Don't let external factors dictate how you feel.

- Take charge of your emotions. Mastering your mindset will yield powerful, noticeable results in your personal and professional life.
- Focus on intentional positivity. Seek out opportunities to reinforce your optimism, even in small ways.

The C Performer: Reluctant Participants

C performers often carry mediocre or negative attitudes, which impacts their productivity, relationships, and overall performance. Their communication and engagement are usually subpar, and this lack of enthusiasm doesn't go unnoticed. While they may achieve acceptable results, they could significantly improve with a better attitude.

Tips for C Performers to Move Up:

- Set a constructive tone early to influence the rest of your day.
- Build stronger relationships with colleagues, friends, or family to enhance your interactions and outlook.
- Acknowledge and appreciate even minor achievements to cultivate a sense of accomplishment.

The Bottom Line

Your attitude is the foundation of your success and happiness. It's your choice, and no one else can control it. A positive mindset creates resilience, fosters stronger relationships, and inspires those around you, while a negative outlook holds you back and diminishes your impact. Whether striving to elevate your performance or maintain excellence, attitude is the key to unlocking your potential and creating a ripple effect of growth and positivity in your personal and professional life. Choose wisely—it starts with you.

2

DEVELOPING A WAKE-UP FRAME OF MIND

Your day truly begins the moment you lift your head off the pillow. That first moment can set the tone for whether you'll have a good, mediocre, or poor day. Yes, circumstances that arise later may play a part, but how you start your day matters. Many factors can influence your morning mindset—perhaps you're battling a minor illness, your children woke you in the middle of the night, you indulged in one too many drinks, or you simply had a restless night of sleep. Whatever the cause, the key is to reduce those negative influences as much as possible to ensure you wake up refreshed and ready. Setting yourself up for a restful night increases your chances of having a productive and positive day.

But remember, the stage for a good day is often set the night before. Going to bed with a positive mindset can make all the difference. If you find yourself struggling to start the day right, take a moment to identify what's consistently holding you back. Then, work to minimize or eliminate those challenges. By doing so, you'll not only improve your mornings, but you'll set yourself up for success every day.

Setting a Morning Routine

Another critical aspect of developing a strong wake-up frame of mind is establishing a consistent morning routine. These small rituals can set a positive tone for the day, whether it's drinking a glass of water, brewing your first cup of coffee, walking the dog, or catching up on the news.

For me, walking the dog early in the morning has become my most valuable thinking time. As an early riser, I started this habit 25 years ago, and it's been immensely beneficial for both my dogs and me. The early hours are quiet, traffic is minimal, and there's little chance for distractions. This routine clears my mind and sets a calm and focused tone for the rest of the day.

Attitude and Morning Performance

How you approach the morning often reflects your overall level of performance.

The A Performer: The Energized Star

An A performer wakes up with a positive mindset and an eagerness to tackle the day. They don't hit the snooze button or dwell on minor discomforts like a restless night or lingering fatigue. Instead, they focus on starting the day with intention and energy, recognizing that a strong attitude can carry them through any challenges. For A performers, even difficult mornings become opportunities to strengthen their resolve. They know that consistency in their wake-up frame of mind is foundational to personal and professional success and productivity.

The B Performer: The Occasional Optimist

B performers generally approach their mornings with a good attitude but may not always start as strong as A performers. They're more likely to hit the snooze button or let minor setbacks—like poor sleep or family interruptions—affect their mood. These factors can sometimes become excuses, setting a negative tone for the day.

Tip to Become an A Performer:

- **Go to bed with intention:** Ending your day with a positive mindset increases the likelihood of waking up refreshed.
- **Wake up a little earlier each day:** By creating a buffer between waking up and starting your responsibilities, you'll feel more in control and prepared for the day ahead.

The C Performer: The Slow Starter

C performers often struggle to wake up with energy or optimism. Their mornings are dominated by excuses—illness, children, or a restless night—which dictate the rest of the day. While they may occasionally feel energized, this is the exception rather than the rule. Their negative wake-up mindset directly impacts their productivity and interactions.

Tips for C Performers to Move Up:

- Identify one or two factors that consistently hold you back from a positive morning and work on addressing them.
- Start small—drink a glass of water, stretch, or take five minutes to reflect on something positive.
- Acknowledge even minor improvements, such as getting out of bed on time or feeling energized. These small wins build momentum for lasting change.

The Bottom Line

Your morning mindset sets the stage for the entire day. How you approach those first moments after waking up reflects not only your attitude but also your level of commitment to success. Whether you're an A Performer who greets the day with positivity and focus, a B Performer who struggles with consistency, or a C Performer battling negativity, your morning routine is an opportunity to shape your future. The key is to take ownership of your mornings. Begin with small, intentional actions that set a positive tone, and remember that the foundation for a good day is often laid the night before. Identify the habits and challenges that hold you back, and work to eliminate them step by step. By prioritizing rest, creating simple rituals, and adopting a proactive mindset, you can transform your mornings and your life.

3

ACHIEVING A HIGH LEVEL OF SELF-ESTEEM

If you want to live a life of fulfillment and purpose, there's one critical foundation you must build—*self-esteem*. A high level of self-esteem is essential for personal growth, relationship success, continuing education, and professional advancement. When you feel good about yourself, that confidence shines through in everything you do, creating a cycle of positive results. The higher your self-esteem, the more confident you become; the more confident you are, the higher your self-esteem rises.

Let's be clear: self-esteem isn't something you're born with. It's developed over time, starting early and continuing throughout life. For some, it begins with the mastery of basic schoolwork or success in extracurricular activities like sports, music, or art. But not everyone starts there—and that's okay. Many A Performers struggled early on in life, but they grew and developed over time, learning to turn their challenges into strengths.

The good news is that self-esteem can always be improved. It doesn't matter where you start; it matters that you're willing to grow. And growth requires intention, focus, and a willingness to develop new habits.

Building Self-Esteem: Key Areas of Focus

There are several key areas you can focus on to enhance your self-esteem. Each one plays a part in building a solid foundation of confidence and self-worth.

- **Practice Self-Compassion**
Let's start with one fundamental truth: *No one is perfect.* Mistakes are part of the human experience, and they always have been. The sooner you accept this, the sooner you can begin to grow. When you recognize your own imperfections and are kind to yourself in the process, you create space for personal growth. Rather than beating yourself up, see your mistakes as opportunities to learn and improve.
- **Set Realistic Goals**
Goal-setting is a powerful tool, but there's a catch: your goals must be realistic. Unrealistic goals lead to frustration, disappointment, and a decline in self-esteem. Break down larger goals into smaller, manageable tasks. Each small victory will build momentum, and momentum leads to confidence. Remember to celebrate

your wins—small celebrations for small victories and bigger celebrations for major milestones. This keeps your journey positive and reinforces your sense of achievement.

- **Challenge Negative Thoughts**
Negative thoughts can be a serious roadblock to self-esteem. They often carry more weight than positive ones because we tend to focus more on what goes wrong than what goes right. Use fact-based reasoning to counter these negative thoughts. Remind yourself of your successes and past achievements. When you challenge negativity with truth, you'll start to weaken its hold on you.

- **Learn from Mistakes**
Mistakes are inevitable, but they don't have to define you. What matters is how you respond to them. Learn from your mistakes, and then let them go. Don't let negative thoughts about past failures dominate your mindset. It's easy to get stuck in a loop of self-doubt, especially if others are critical of you. But remember, the opinions of others don't have to determine your self-worth.

- **Focus on Your Strengths**
Each of us has unique strengths and talents. Spend time identifying what you're good at and focus on those areas. Don't waste time comparing yourself to others—focus on being the best version of *yourself*. When you operate

to your strengths, you'll produce positive results, and those results will build your confidence even more.

- **Take Care of Yourself**
  Physical health and self-esteem are closely linked. Take care of your body with good sleep, proper nutrition, and regular exercise. Healthy sleep patterns help you wake up with a clear mind, ready to tackle the day. Eating well fuels your energy, and regular exercise—whether a gym routine or something as simple as walking—boosts your mood and overall well-being.

- **Avoid Comparisons**
  One of the most dangerous habits for your self-esteem is comparing yourself to others. I live by an old saying: *"Try to be yourself; everyone else is taken."* This simple truth frees you from the burden of comparison. You have unique talents and strengths, and so do others. Focus on being the best version of yourself, and let others do the same. You'll find peace, confidence, and a greater sense of self-worth when you stop comparing.

A Performers: Confidence and High Self-Esteem

A Performers consistently operate with high levels of self-esteem, projecting confidence built on habits that support growth and success. Many of these habits are established early in life, but A Performers continue to refine and strengthen them over time. They see mistakes as opportunities to learn and adapt, always seeking ways to improve without letting setbacks define them. What truly sets A Performers apart is their intentional focus. They set aggressive yet realistic goals, pushing themselves to achieve them while staying grounded in what's achievable. Rather than fixating on weaknesses, they double down on their strengths, sharpening their skills to excel in their roles. This clarity of focus allows them to approach challenges with confidence and determination.

A Performers also prioritize self-care and perspective. They know that physical and mental well-being are essential to peak performance, so they prioritize staying healthy. Perhaps most importantly, they avoid comparisons, focusing instead on their journey and trusting their unique abilities. This self-assured mindset enables them to thrive and inspire others around them.

Personally, I can relate to this category. From winning tennis competitions to graduating with honors from Georgia Tech, I've seen firsthand how strong self-esteem can drive success. But like all A Performers, I've learned that perfection is not the goal—it's about consistently putting in the work and learning from each step.

B Performers: Solid, but with Room to Grow

B Performers often experience moments of high self-esteem, but it's not as consistent as it could be. They may excel in some areas while struggling in others, leading to a range of performance. Their self-esteem fluctuates based on circumstances—sometimes, they feel confident, and other times they doubt themselves.

Tips to Become an A Performer:

- Review the key areas listed above and determine where you're falling short. Is it setting realistic goals? Practicing self-compassion? Identifying these areas is the first step to improvement.
- Focus on making small adjustments in the areas where you can see the most immediate impact. It doesn't take huge shifts to see results—sometimes, a few small changes can make all the difference.
- Spend time with people who exhibit high self-esteem and confidence. Learn from their habits and mindsets, and incorporate what works for you.

C Performers: Struggling with Low Self-Esteem

C Performers regularly experience low self-esteem and may struggle with confidence in most areas of their life. They may occasionally rise to the level of a B or even an A Performer, but these moments are fleeting. C Performers are often weighed down by negative thoughts, self-doubt, and comparisons to others.

Tips for C Performers to Move Up:

- Start by identifying the negative thoughts and habits that are holding you back. Are you overly critical of yourself? Do you set unrealistic goals that lead to frustration? Acknowledge these patterns so you can begin to change them.
- Everyone has something they're good at. Spend time discovering your strengths and focusing on them. This will help build your confidence and give you a foundation to grow.
- Don't try to overhaul your life overnight. Make small, positive changes and build on those successes over time. Each step forward will contribute to a stronger sense of self-esteem.

The Bottom Line

Self-esteem is the foundation for personal growth, confidence, and success. Whether you're already an A Performer or working to improve, the journey to high self-esteem never ends. It's about constantly growing, learning from mistakes, and building on your strengths. Remember, you are unique, and you have strengths that no one else does. Focus on developing those strengths, care for yourself, and don't waste time comparing yourself to others. When you do, you'll find that your self-esteem and confidence will grow in ways you never thought possible. Keep pushing forward, and watch your life transform.

4

DEVELOPING AND MAINTAINING HEALTHY RELATIONSHIPS

Healthy relationships are the glue that holds our lives together. Whether personal or professional, strong interpersonal connections are essential for success and fulfillment. No one is an island—we rely on human interaction to thrive, build community, and achieve our goals. Relationships impact every area of life, from family and friends to colleagues and clients, and nurturing them requires intentional effort.

The Importance of Relationships

Relationships evolve as life unfolds. Some last a lifetime, while others are fleeting. Depending on the circumstances, they can be strong and steady or fragile and strained. Despite the endless combinations, one truth remains: relationships matter.

One piece of advice resonates: relationships work best when both parties put in 60% effort. Relationships can grow stronger and last longer when people consistently go above and beyond.

Family Relationships

Family relationships can be some of the most rewarding and challenging connections in life. We've all heard the saying: *You can pick your friends but can't pick your family.* This truth underscores both the joy and the complexity of family ties.

For example, my wife Kathy and I come from families with unique and complex dynamics. Between us, we had nine parents due to multiple divorces and remarriages in our families. Managing these relationships was often challenging, but we learned to navigate the complexities with grace over time. How did we handle the challenge? Kathy and I decided to become "Switzerland." We maintained neutrality, avoided gossip, and focused on fostering positive connections with as many family members as possible. When conflicts arose, we aimed to make amends and improve strained relationships. The key lesson is to identify the relationships that matter most—spouse or significant other, children, parents, and siblings—and invest your time and energy into keeping them healthy.

Personal Relationships

Beyond family, personal relationships are a vital part of life. From childhood friends to neighbors and social circles, these connections provide joy, support, and companionship. While some friendships may fade over time, others remain strong and evolve with life's changes. However, not all personal relationships are smooth. Kathy, for example, experienced challenges with some strong friendships that ended due to misunderstandings or conflict. These experiences taught us that maintaining healthy personal relationships requires effort, empathy, and, sometimes, the willingness to move on when a relationship no longer serves both parties. The key lesson is to foster relationships that enrich your life and bring mutual satisfaction. When a relationship becomes strained, assess its long-term value. If it's worth saving, take steps to rebuild it. If not, let it go quietly and respectfully.

Professional Relationships

Dealing with, working with

Professional relationships are equally important. Whether in the workplace, in volunteer roles, or in social organizations, these connections often determine long-term success. Sincerity, trustworthiness, and effective communication are the foundation of productive professional relationships. Building these relationships isn't just about collaboration; it's about creating a positive environment where people want to work with you. If you are dependable, clear in your communication, and open to feedback, you will foster professional relationships that stand the test of time.

A Performers: Routinely Foster Healthy Relationships

A Performers excel at fostering and sustaining healthy relationships across all areas of life. They approach connections with consistency, a positive attitude, and strong communication skills, ensuring their relationships remain meaningful and productive. When challenges arise, A Performers rely on the strength of these bonds, demonstrating resilience and commitment to maintaining harmony and mutual respect.

One of the key strengths of A Performers is their ability to build and nurture relationships in both personal and professional spheres. They prioritize high-quality connections, even in difficult circumstances, and understand the value of balancing clear communication with active listening. Their ability to adapt and empathize makes them dependable and sought-after in all types of interactions.

Consistency is crucial to maintaining A-level performance in relationships. A Performers use the same habits and principles of positive engagement across all areas of life, creating stability and trust. They also focus on mastering effective communication by expressing their thoughts clearly while being attentive and responsive listeners. These practices not only strengthen relationships but also ensure long-term success in personal and professional endeavors.

B Performers: Fair Weather and Inconsistent

B Performers can develop healthy relationships, but their success is often situational. They maintain strong connections when favorable, but these relationships may falter under pressure or during challenging circumstances. This inconsistency can limit the depth and resilience of their interactions, particularly when adversity arises. Additionally, B Performers often prioritize certain relationships, such as professional ones, while neglecting others, like family or personal connections, creating an imbalance that may lead to strained dynamics over time.

While B Performers show reliability in specific areas and maintain solid relationships in good conditions, their areas for improvement are clear. To elevate their performance, they must focus on strengthening relationships during tough times and striving for balance across all aspects of life. By addressing these weaknesses, B Performers can create more stable and enduring connections, both personally and professionally.

Tips to Become an A Performer:

- Develop and apply strong habits for maintaining healthy relationships in personal, family, and professional settings.
- Enhance your ability to share thoughts and ideas in a way that is easy to understand and impactful.

- Focus on truly hearing and understanding others to build trust and strengthen connections.

C Performers: Struggle with Healthy Relationships

C Performers often struggle with building and maintaining relationships across all areas of life. Family ties may become strained due to unresolved conflicts or lack of effort, leading to distance from those closest to them. Personal friendships often lack depth or consistency, and acquaintances may drift away over time. In professional settings, weak communication skills and limited engagement can result in underperformance and missed opportunities for collaboration or advancement.

These relational challenges create a cycle of isolation, hindering growth in both personal and professional spheres. Without meaningful connections, C Performers may struggle to foster trust, achieve their goals, or feel supported in their endeavors. Addressing these issues requires intentional effort to strengthen bonds and improve communication at home and in the workplace.

Tips for C Performers to Move Up:

- Identify and address the factors contributing to poor relationships, such as attitude or communication gaps.

- Learn from those who excel at building relationships, and apply their methods to improve your own.
- Work on being a better family member, friend, or colleague by focusing on one or two areas for improvement.

The Bottom Line

Relationships are the foundation of personal and professional success. Whether with family, friends, or colleagues, strong and healthy connections enrich our lives and help us navigate life's challenges. Your challenge is to reach out to two people—family, personal, or professional—with whom you've had a strained relationship. Take the first step to mend fences and rebuild those connections. Even if the outcome isn't perfect, you'll grow from the experience and demonstrate your commitment to healthy relationships.

morgan & morgan ad

5

MASTERING COMMUNICATION FOR PERSONAL AND PROFESSIONAL SUCCESS

Communication is the lifeblood of all relationships—personal and professional. If you want to build meaningful connections and achieve success, mastering communication is essential. We communicate in countless ways: face-to-face conversations, emails, texts, phone calls, social media, and more. Each interaction is an opportunity to connect, clarify, and strengthen relationships.

Strong communication enhances your life and the lives of those around you. But here's the key: **people aren't mind readers.** Clear, concise communication is essential if you want to be understood and achieve your desired outcomes. Without it, even the best intentions can fall short.

Two Halves of Communication

Effective communication involves two equally important skills: **conveying your message clearly** and **being a good listener.**

- **Clear, Crisp, and Concise Communication**
  Your message must be clear and direct when you communicate—whether verbally or in writing. Provide the necessary details, set expectations for performance, and establish specific timeframes for action. This clarity lets others respond more effectively, ensuring positive outcomes for everyone involved.

- **The Art of Listening**
  Being a good listener is just as important as delivering a clear message. Listening requires intentional focus and respect for the speaker. To listen well, maintain positive body language, especially eye contact. Also, avoid distractions like phones or wandering thoughts and show you're fully engaged in the conversation.

People notice whether you're a good listener, impacting the quality of your relationships. Listening creates trust and opens the door to greater productivity and stronger connections.

Communication Is a Lifelong Skill

Good communication starts early in life. Babies cry to express hunger or pain. Toddlers throw tantrums or shout to get what they want, quickly learning what works. By adulthood, our methods of communication have grown more sophisticated, but the fundamentals remain the same. Good communication habits will serve you well in personal and professional relationships. Poor habits, however, can create frustration and hold you back. The good news? **Habits can change.** Start by identifying one or two areas to improve. Work on those, see the positive results and let progress build on progress. Every small improvement enhances your ability to connect and succeed. Progress leads to more progress!

Adapting to Others' Preferences

Effective communicators understand the value of adapting to the preferences of others. Some people prefer a phone call, others like texting, and some favor email. Cater to their preferences, and you'll strengthen relationships and improve the overall experience—whether with family, coworkers, or clients.

A Performers: Masters of Communication

A Performers excel in communication because they approach it with clarity, respect, and a strong sense of purpose. They initiate conversations to ensure others understand exactly what's needed, leaving no room for ambiguity. Recognizing that people aren't mind readers, they articulate their needs clearly and thoughtfully, fostering productive interactions. Their communication isn't just effective—it's intentional, tailored to the situation, and designed to build trust and understanding.

Timely communication is another hallmark of A Performers. They understand how to prioritize responses based on urgency. When faced with critical issues, such as a crisis at work, they respond immediately to keep operations running smoothly. They ensure responses are thoughtful and deliberate for less time-sensitive matters, like weighing options or making non-urgent decisions, balancing efficiency with quality. This ability to manage communication priorities sets them apart as leaders who drive results through effective dialogue.

B Performers: Decent but Inconsistent

B performers generally communicate well but lack the consistency of A performers. They respond inconsistently, sometimes frustrating others. They also assume others understand their needs without providing enough detail.

Tips to Become an A Performer:

- Don't delay calls, texts, or emails longer than necessary.
- Provide enough detail to ensure everyone is on the same page.
- The more effort you put into communication, the better the results you'll see.

C Performers: Struggling with Communication

C performers often struggle the most with communication. They respond slowly or not at all, which others may perceive as rude or dismissive. They also avoid initiating conversations and waiting for others to engage with them. Over time, poor communication habits cause frustration and lead others to avoid working with them. But there's hope!

Tips for C Performers to Move Up:

- Commit to responding to every email, text, or call—even if it takes time.
- Practice initiating communication instead of waiting for others to reach out.
- Recognize that people aren't mind readers. Be clear and provide enough detail to resolve issues efficiently.

A PERFORMER, A ENVIRONMENT

The Bottom Line

Mastering communication is essential for personal and professional success. When you communicate clearly, listen actively, and adapt to the needs of others, you'll strengthen relationships, open new opportunities, and achieve greater results. Communication is a skill that affects every part of your life, and like all skills, it can be improved. Whether you're aiming to be an A Performer or moving up from a B or C, the principles are the same: respond promptly, be clear, and adapt your communication style to meet the needs of those around you. When you do, you'll see relationships improve, opportunities grow, and success follow. And becoming a GREAT listener will pay very good dividends.

6

START THE DAY CONSISTENTLY AND STAY ENGAGED

Let's talk about how you start your day. Whether you're working in an office, in the field, or remotely, how you begin your day sets the tone for everything that follows. If your day is supposed to start at 8:00 a.m., then start at 8:00—*not* 9:00, *not* 9:30. *Be available. Be prepared.* This may seem simple, but it's fundamental to your personal and professional productivity and success.

Starting your day on time is more than just a logistical detail—it's a signal to yourself and others that you're committed. It creates consistency in your routine and sets the stage for a productive day. How often have you gotten a late start and felt like you couldn't catch up? When that happens, it doesn't just affect that day. It spills over the next day, creating a cycle of stress and missed opportunities. On the other hand, when you start on time, prepared and ready, you set yourself up to be productive, focused, and engaged.

The Ripple Effect of Consistency

Consistency is key. People notice when you make it a habit to start your day on time. Your colleagues and leaders see that you are reliable, dependable, and committed. They associate you with high professionalism and know they can count on you to be there when needed. And here's the powerful part: when people see you as dependable, they seek you out. They engage with you more frequently. They trust you. And that trust opens doors for opportunities and growth.

Now, let's flip that coin. People notice that you're inconsistent, routinely start late, or are unprepared. They will start to see you as unreliable, and that perception will affect how often they come to you for important tasks or opportunities. Being late or unavailable isn't just a minor inconvenience; it directly impacts your reputation and future growth.

It's Not Just About the Start—
It's About the Finish, Too

Starting the day on time is only part of the equation. Your commitment to consistency has to carry through the entire day. Are you available and engaged when people need you throughout the workday? When you say you'll be available at a certain time, are you actually there? Being consistently available builds trust—and trust is the cornerstone of strong professional relationships.

And here's the often overlooked part: how you *finish* the day is just as important as how you start it. Are you still engaged when the clock hits 5:00 or 6:00? Are you wrapping up your work with the same focus and energy as you started? Just as starting the day strong sets the tone for the hours ahead, finishing the day well sets you up for success the next day. Remember, the end of the day is when many people check in, wrap up projects, and set the stage for tomorrow. Finishing strong is crucial for keeping momentum.

A Performers: Consistent, Reliable, and Always Prepared

A Performers have mastered this principle. They are known for starting their day on time and being consistently available. When the clock strikes 8:00, they're ready—focused, prepared, and engaged. This level of consistency is no accident; it's a habit they've built over time.

A Performers don't just show up on time; they stay engaged for the full day. They know that productivity isn't about short bursts of effort—it's about sustained focus throughout the day. And they understand that being available during off-hours, when necessary, makes them dependable leaders and teammates.

But A Performers also have a mindset of *ownership*. They don't let minor setbacks or distractions keep them from staying on track. Even in challenging circumstances, they maintain consistency, knowing that others count on them. This consistency is why their peers and superiors so highly value them.

B Performers: Solid, But Inconsistent

B Performers are generally reliable, but there are times when they slip. They usually start the day on time, but there are occasional mornings when they're not fully prepared, or they arrive a little late. These small inconsistencies may not seem like a big deal, but they can add up and affect how they are perceived.

B Performers work a full day, but sometimes their engagement fluctuates. They may slack off for an hour here or there, and their availability during off-hours can be hit or miss. This is understandable, especially for those with young families or other commitments, but it's something to be mindful of. Business leaders recognize the balance between work and life, but maintaining consistency as much as possible is crucial for moving from a B to an A Performer.

Tips to Become an A Performer:

- If you find yourself occasionally slipping in your start time or engagement, take time to reflect. Are there specific patterns or reasons for these lapses? Once you recognize them, you can work to minimize them.
- Spend time with those who consistently start their day strong. Learn from their routines,

- Don't let an off day derail you. If you fall behind one day, don't let that become a pattern. Reset, refocus, and start strong the next day.

C Performers: Struggling with Consistency

C Performers, unfortunately, struggle with starting their day on time and maintaining consistency throughout the day. They might start at 8:00 sometimes, but more often than not, they're late. Maybe it's 8:15 or 8:30, or worse, closer to 9:00. And while those small delays might not seem significant at the moment, they create a perception of unreliability. C Performers are also often seen as inconsistent. Others notice when they're late or unavailable, affecting their ability to build strong relationships with their team. Over time, this inconsistency can lead to isolation, as colleagues avoid relying on them for important tasks or projects.

Tips for C Performers to Move Up:

- What's causing your late starts or lack of availability? Is it your routine, distractions, or something else? Once you understand the barriers, you can begin to address them.
- Establish a routine that helps you start the day on time, every time. Whether setting an earlier

alarm or preparing the night before, find what works for you.
- **Ask a colleague or mentor to hold you accountable for your start times.** Sometimes, a little external motivation is all it takes to create new habits.

The Bottom Line

At the end of the day, how you start and finish your day matters. Your ability to show up on time, be available, and stay engaged isn't just about productivity—it's about building trust and reliability. When you're consistent, people notice. They see you as someone they can count on, and that reputation creates new opportunities for growth and advancement. So, ask yourself: Are you starting your day on time? Are you finishing strong? If not, what small changes can you make to become more consistent? Remember, success isn't about one big effort—it's about the small, consistent actions you take every single day.

7

STRONG WORK ETHIC PRODUCES GOOD RESULTS

When it comes to achieving long-term success, both personally and professionally, there's one quality that stands out above the rest: *A strong work ethic.* Your work ethic is the driving force behind everything you do. It determines how well you manage your relationships, your responsibilities, and, ultimately, your results. If you want to reach your full potential in life, it starts with how much effort you're willing to put in.

A Strong Work Ethic in Personal Life

Let's start with the personal side. Many people don't often think of their personal relationships as requiring a "work ethic," but in truth, they do. Every relationship—whether with your spouse or significant other, children, parents, or friends—requires effort. Healthy relationships don't just happen. They require intentional investment.

I've often heard that relationships should operate on a 60/40 principle—each person should aim to put in 60% effort. Why? Because when you give more than you take, you create a strong, productive, and long-lasting relationship. I fundamentally believe this is true. Whether it's spending quality time with your family, being there for your friends, or supporting your loved ones through tough times, the effort you put in will directly impact the quality of those relationships.

A Strong Work Ethic in Professional Life

Now, let's talk about the professional side. A strong work ethic is absolutely critical for long-term success in any career. It influences how you approach your job, your relationships with colleagues, and the quality of the work you produce. It's not just about the hours you put in—it's about *how* you use those hours.

A strong work ethic manifests in many ways. It's about developing strong relationships with your team and contributing to a positive work environment. It's about taking quiet time to think strategically about your work, engaging fully in meetings, and bringing fresh, healthy perspectives to the table. It's waking up with a positive attitude, ready to face the day, and constantly seeking opportunities for personal and professional growth.

No one is perfect, and no one can have a 100% capture rate on all these factors all the time. But the effort you put into developing these habits consistently

STRONG WORK ETHIC PRODUCES GOOD RESULTS

will determine your trajectory. The more you work on your ethics, the more success will naturally follow.

A Performers: Leading with a Strong Work Ethic

A Performers stand out because they have a work ethic that drives them to produce positive results consistently. Whether it's an innate trait or something they've deliberately cultivated, A Performers take pride in their ability to stay focused on their objectives, no matter the circumstances.

What makes them special is that they don't shy away from difficult situations. In fact, they often welcome challenges. Why? Because overcoming adversity fuels their growth. It's the "Mt. Everest" mentality—*I'm going to conquer this because I can*. For A Performers, the tougher the problem, the greater the opportunity to prove their resilience and commitment.

You can see these qualities develop early in life. A Performers attack learning opportunities with enthusiasm. They understand the value of practice in sports—putting in the hours even when no one's watching. In artistic endeavors like music, dance, or theatre, they always look for ways to improve, starting new projects and pushing their limits. This relentless pursuit of excellence is what sets A Performers apart. They don't just work hard—they work smart. They stay focused, adapt to changing circumstances, and continually seek ways to grow. This mindset is what leads to long-term success.

B Performers: Good, But Room to Grow

B Performers typically have a decent work ethic and can produce solid results. There are moments when their engagement spikes, and they show brilliance in their work. However, the issue with B Performers is that their level of effort can fluctuate.

In one situation, they may fully commit and produce excellent results. In another, they may only engage modestly, producing acceptable but not exceptional outcomes. At times, they may even coast, doing just enough to get by. This inconsistency can hold them back from reaching their full potential. B Performers have the foundation to become A Performers, but they need to develop greater consistency. It's about adopting a mindset where every situation is an opportunity to engage fully and bring your best effort.

Tips to Become an A Performer:

- Approach each new situation with the mindset that you will put in the work to achieve great results.
- Find people who exhibit the strong work ethic you admire. Engage with them regularly to learn their habits and perspectives.

- Don't settle for "good enough"—even in small or unimportant tasks. Treat each one as an opportunity to prove your commitment to excellence.

C Performers: Struggling with Work Ethic

C Performers, on the other hand, often struggle to maintain even a basic level of work ethic. Their motivation is low, and their results reflect that lack of effort. The work they produce is often late, incomplete, or of poor quality. It's common for their work to need additional oversight, corrections, or revisions by others, which can create frustration within teams.

C Performers are often known for doing just enough to get by. You might hear this referred to as "working the wage," where individuals do only the bare minimum required. This attitude not only limits their personal growth but also damages relationships with colleagues and supervisors. Over time, people begin to avoid working with them, leaving them isolated and with limited opportunities for advancement.

Tips for C Performers to Move Up:

- Wake up earlier, start your day with intention, and tackle your responsibilities head-on. Small changes can have a big impact on your overall work ethic.

- Find someone with a strong work ethic and ask for mentorship. By learning from those who excel, you can adopt better habits and improve your performance.
- Focus on improving one area at a time. As you start to see positive results, you'll build momentum and confidence in your ability to improve.

The Bottom Line

At the end of the day, your work ethic is the foundation upon which your success is built. Whether in your personal relationships or professional endeavors, your effort directly impacts the results you get. The good news? A strong work ethic isn't something you're born with—it's something you can develop. If you want to be an A Performer, it starts with deciding to engage fully, even when it's hard. It's about owning your responsibilities, taking pride in your work, and constantly seeking ways to improve. Whether at the top of your game or working your way up, the key to long-term success is consistently putting in the effort. With a strong work ethic, there's no limit to what you can achieve. Are you willing to put in the work?

8

BE A PROBLEM SOLVER

The world is full of problems—and it needs problem solvers. Whether in your personal life or professional career, being an effective problem solver is fundamental. It's not just about doing your job; it's about helping others be more productive and contributing to the greater good.

The best problem solvers approach issues with an open mind. They don't just see obstacles; they see challenges to overcome and opportunities to grow. Turning a problem into a challenge and then turning that challenge into an opportunity is the hallmark of great problem-solving.

The Nature of Problems

Problems are a universal experience, arising in all environments and circumstances. They range in severity and complexity, but one thing is certain: problems are a constant part of life. Merriam-Webster defines a problem as "a question raised for inquiry, consideration, or solution" and "a source of perplexity, distress, or vexation."

Every workplace, industry, and personal setting encounters problems, and addressing them effectively is critical to success. For example:

- **In business environments,** challenges like employee retention, supply chain issues, and financial management can significantly impact productivity and morale.
- **In specialized fields like land development and homebuilding,** unique problems include zoning regulations, material shortages, labor constraints, and weather delays.

In any context, the ability to recognize, evaluate, and solve problems is essential for growth and progress.

Turn Problems into Challenges

The first step in solving a problem is to reframe it as a challenge. This subtle psychological shift changes how we view the issue. A problem may feel like a burden, but a challenge is an opportunity to rise to the occasion.

Merriam-Webster defines a challenge as "a stimulating task or problem." The word "stimulating" is key—it highlights the importance of motivation and engagement in the problem-solving process. When we feel stimulated by a challenge, we are more likely to apply focus and creativity to reach a positive outcome.

Why Reframing Works

When you approach an issue as a challenge, it energizes you to act. It also reduces procrastination as the task becomes more engaging and less daunting. It focuses your attention on solutions, not obstacles. Here's the reality: Not all problems need to be addressed. Some resolve themselves or lose relevance over time. So, your goal is to identify and tackle the issues that matter by reframing them as challenges that deserve your attention.

Turn Challenges into Opportunities

The next step in effective problem-solving is turning challenges into opportunities. This is where the process shifts into a mindset of progress and growth. Merriam-Webster defines an opportunity as "a favorable juncture of circumstances" and "a good chance for advancement or progress." When you view a challenge as an opportunity, you position yourself to solve the problem and benefit from the solution. Your mindset becomes more positive, and the path to resolution becomes clearer.

Example:

Years ago, I owned a floating house on a lake in North Georgia. The U.S. Army Corps of Engineers raised concerns about wastewater discharge from these homes, requiring a solution. Leveraging my home-building experience, I turned this problem into a challenge by researching and designing a custom holding tank system for the water. The opportunity came when my house became the prototype for a solution that benefitted all 32 floating homes in the area. By addressing the issue with an open mind, collaboration, and action, the problem was resolved effectively.

Tips for Being a Good Problem Solver

Here are practical strategies for developing your problem-solving skills:

- **Start with your responsibilities.** Focus on addressing your core responsibilities effectively and on time.
- **Assess your capacity.** Determine whether you have the time and resources to solve a problem yourself or if it's better to delegate.
- **Leverage strengths and weaknesses.** Understand your abilities and those of your team to decide how best to contribute to a solution.

- **Communicate clearly.** Share your needs and expectations with colleagues and partners. Remember, they aren't mind readers.
- **Bring solutions, not just problems.** When raising an issue, propose potential solutions to demonstrate initiative and focus on resolution.
- **Listen to feedback.** Be open to suggestions from others. They might offer the solution you need.

Communication's Role in Problem Solving

Effective communication is critical to addressing problems. Whether collaborating with teammates or working with external partners, clear communication ensures everyone is aligned and working toward the same goal. Remember to be concise when outlining the problem, provide actionable details, listen to feedback, and adapt accordingly.

A Performers: Masters of Problem Solving

A Performers excel because they maintain open minds and seek out new ideas. They don't settle for the status quo; instead, they challenge old methods and look for innovative solutions. When faced with challenges, A Performers view them as opportunities for growth and progress. They tend to be open to new ideas, willing to learn, and proactively seek better methods and approaches.

B Performers:
Reliable but Hesitant to Change

B Performers are solid problem solvers who deliver reliable results. However, they often stick to familiar routines, even when they may not be the most efficient. While their methods are effective in predictable scenarios, they risk stagnation when faced with new or complex challenges.

B Performers are also dependable and consistent in their approach, often achieving good results in familiar situations. However, they hesitate when stepping outside their comfort zones and may overlook new or innovative solutions that could lead to greater efficiency or success.

Tips to Become an A Performer:

- When facing a familiar problem, ask yourself, "Is there a better way?" Explore alternative approaches.
- Collaborate with people who think differently. A new viewpoint can reveal solutions you might have missed.
- Just because something has worked before isn't the best solution now. Stay flexible and open to change.

C Performers: Stuck in Old Patterns

C Performers struggle with problem solving because they resist change and rely on outdated methods. Their reluctance to adapt or accept feedback often results in repeated mistakes and unproductive outcomes. This resistance not only limits their growth but also frustrates those around them. C Performers often rely on outdated methods, even when those methods prove ineffective, and they struggle to accept feedback or consider new ideas. Additionally, they tend to avoid initiating change or proactively seeking solutions, which can hinder their growth and frustrate those around them.

Tips for C Performers to Move Up:

- Step out of your comfort zone and experiment with different problem-solving approaches.
- Accept feedback and new ideas without becoming defensive. You don't have to agree with everything, but you might learn something valuable.
- Recognizing that no one has all the answers is the first step toward meaningful improvement.

The Bottom Line

Solving problems is one of the most valuable skills you can develop. By keeping an open mind, reframing problems as challenges, and transforming challenges into opportunities, you position yourself for personal and professional success. Life will always present obstacles, but how you approach them makes all the difference. With the right mindset, effective communication, and a willingness to grow, you'll become not just a problem solver—but a problem solver who inspires and empowers those around you.

9

IDENTIFY AND DEVELOP SKILL SETS

Identifying and developing your core skill sets is essential to both professional and personal growth. Everyone has strengths and weaknesses; the key to achieving lasting success is spending time in areas of strength while managing or improving weaker areas when possible. In this chapter, we'll explore categories of skills and discuss how to focus on them effectively.

Understanding How You Spend Your Time

To be productive for yourself, your team, and your organization, it's critical to understand where your time is best spent. While every role has some tasks that may not align perfectly with individual strengths, the goal is to work with managers and colleagues to find a balance that maximizes contributions.

This Focus Extends Beyond Work: Personal Skills Matter Too

At home, just as in the workplace, identifying each person's strengths can lead to better results. For instance, one partner might excel at managing finances, while the other is better at organizing. Modern family dynamics show that tasks traditionally associated with one gender can be handled by either partner based on skill, not stereotypes.

Exploring Key Skill Categories

- **Math and Numerical Skills**: Many professions, like accounting, engineering, and medicine, rely heavily on strong numerical abilities. If math is your strength, lean into it for both professional and household tasks that require accuracy and analysis.
- **Artistic and Creative Skills**: For roles in marketing, design, and other creative fields, an eye for color and design is invaluable. These skills can be applied at home to activities like decorating, planning events, or helping with creative school projects.
- **Musical Skills**: Musical aptitude can be professionally beneficial in industries needing ambiance, like retail or hospitality. On a personal level, music brings value to family gatherings

or events, so let those with a natural musical ear take the lead.
- **Writing Skills**: Strong writing skills are essential in professions that require clear communication, like marketing, law, or education. If you're proficient in writing, focus on tasks that involve crafting messages or drafting documents.
- **Computer and Social Media Skills**: Digital competence is vital in today's business environment, from using software to managing online presence. Those with strong tech skills should embrace digital responsibilities, while others may want to improve or delegate these tasks.
- **Athletic Skills**: For those drawn to sports, professions in coaching, fitness, or sports broadcasting can be fulfilling. On a personal level, identify enjoyable sports for yourself or your family and engage in those for recreation and exercise.

The Lifelong Pursuit of Skills

Your skill sets will evolve over time. Whether you're naturally inclined toward specific tasks or need guidance to improve, try to focus on areas where you're already proficient. Open-mindedness and experimentation can reveal surprising talents or interests, enhancing both personal and professional satisfaction.

A Performers: Focusing on Strengths Early

A Performers excel because they recognize their strengths early and actively seek opportunities that align with those abilities. They understand that excelling in everything is unrealistic, so they prioritize their strongest areas, building a solid foundation for long-term success. This focus allows A Performers to develop mastery and consistently deliver high-quality results in both professional and personal spheres.

A Performers excel by proactively identifying and leveraging their strengths, focusing on skill areas that lead to impactful outcomes. They prioritize what they do best and consistently apply these strengths to achieve meaningful growth and sustained success in both personal and professional settings.

B Performers: Consistent Skills Needing Focus

B Performers have the potential to excel but may initially struggle to identify their strongest skills. They tend to dabble in multiple areas rather than narrow their focus, hindering their progress. By concentrating on a few key areas and seeking input from managers or mentors, B Performers can refine their strengths and become more consistent in their performance.

B Performers demonstrate reliability and competence in specific areas and are receptive to guidance and feedback, which helps them refine their skills and work toward greater consistency and improvement.

IDENTIFY AND DEVELOP SKILL SETS

Tips to Become an A Performer:

- Identify your top two or three skills and dedicate time to refining them.
- Collaborate with trusted mentors or colleagues to gain clarity on where you excel and how to improve further.
- Once you've mastered your core skills, explore complementary areas to broaden your expertise and increase your impact.

C Performers: Developing a Starting Point

C Performers often face challenges in identifying their strengths, leading to frustration and limited progress. However, everyone has a starting point. By focusing on one or two areas of interest and committing to improvement, C Performers can gradually develop their skills. With the right guidance and accountability, they can build confidence and begin the journey toward higher performance.

C Performers also often struggle to identify and leverage their strengths, leading to a lack of focus and inconsistency in skill development, which can hinder their growth and progress. Overcoming these challenges requires intentional effort and a willingness to explore new areas of improvement.

Tips for C Performers to Move Up:

- Focus on small, manageable goals to build momentum.
- Work with someone who can provide feedback and encouragement.
- Recognize and reward even small improvements to stay motivated.

The Bottom Line

Your strengths are the foundation for long-term growth and success, serving as the cornerstone for achieving your goals. By identifying and prioritizing the areas where you excel and committing to ongoing development, you can create a lasting impact professionally and personally. Strengthening these core abilities not only boosts your confidence but also enhances the value you bring to your team, organization, and relationships. Whether you're an A, B, or C Performer, dedicating time and effort to refine your strengths today will unlock greater accomplishments, open new opportunities, and lead to a deeper sense of satisfaction in the future.

10

TAKE ON ADDITIONAL TASKS

Taking on additional responsibilities is a powerful way to grow professionally and personally. Every role comes with defined duties, but in dynamic work environments, extra tasks are always waiting for someone to step up. It's noticed and appreciated when you're that person, no matter your position in the organization.

When a new task or project arises, do you jump in or wait for someone else to take the lead? This choice applies to everyone—ownership, management, and staff alike. Taking the initiative consistently—not just occasionally—demonstrates a commitment to excellence that others notice and value.

Being Proactive Creates an Opportunity

Seizing opportunities to help or support team members enhances current performance and sets the stage for growth, advancement, and even increased income. A mindset of active participation shows that you're ready to contribute, not only in your role but also in any other areas where you can add value. If you consistently volunteer, others will see you as a team player who is dependable and engaged.

Remember, if you don't step up, that also gets noticed. So, consider: who do you want to be in the eyes of your colleagues?

Balance Your Commitments

While stepping up is valuable, balancing it with your existing responsibilities is essential. Taking on too much can dilute your effectiveness in all areas. The goal is quality over quantity—focusing on a few key tasks and doing them well. A disciplined approach, focusing on "two things, not ten," helps prevent overload and ensures the best possible outcomes.

Build Situational Awareness

Awareness of what's happening around you enhances your ability to choose when to step up. Understanding ongoing projects and team dynamics lets you judge when and how to help most effectively. Routine meetings offer a great place to identify these opportunities. In such settings, staying attuned and actively contributing sets a positive example and shows others you're engaged.

In some environments, you might find yourself "voluntold" rather than volunteering—assigned additional responsibilities when necessary. Both approaches have value, and proactively volunteering gives you more influence over the tasks you assume. But remember, even when voluntary, embracing the task with a positive attitude strengthens your reputation.

This Approach Extends Beyond the Work

The principles of taking on additional tasks apply at home as well. Relationships thrive when all parties contribute fully. In a healthy partnership, everyone takes on what's needed—even outside their comfort zone. Household tasks, family responsibilities, and shared goals benefit from everyone putting in that extra effort. Think back to childhood—many of us started with chores and responsibilities, learning the value of helping out early. This mindset carries over to adult life and professional environments.

The Role of Additional Responsibilities

Taking on extra tasks and responsibilities is an excellent way to demonstrate commitment, build trust, and open doors for personal and professional growth. However, the willingness to step up and the ability to manage additional responsibilities effectively vary by performance level.

A Performers: Proactively Taking on More

A Performers consistently assess their capacity and step up to take on extra tasks when possible. They understand that doing so demonstrates their dedication and creates opportunities for growth and advancement. A Performers excel at managing additional responsibilities by maintaining open communication about their workload and offering thoughtful suggestions to ensure responsibilities are handled efficiently.

A Performers excel at taking on additional responsibilities because they proactively seek out tasks that align with their capacity and goals. They don't wait to be asked; instead, they look for opportunities to add value and contribute meaningfully. A Performers are also skilled communicators, openly discussing their workload and responsibilities to ensure that expectations are clear and achievable. This transparency allows them to manage their tasks effectively while maintaining trust with their colleagues and managers. Most importantly, they view extra responsibilities not as burdens but as opportunities for growth, leveraging these tasks to expand their skills, enhance their contributions, and position themselves for greater success.

B Performers: Stepping Up Selectively

B Performers are reliable and step up to take on additional tasks when they fit their routine and don't strain their current responsibilities. While this approach sometimes works, it can limit their growth when immediate or unexpected action is required. By becoming more proactive and intentional, B Performers can take on additional responsibilities that expand their capabilities and demonstrate greater commitment.

B Performers are willing to take on extra responsibilities as long as they feel the tasks are manageable within their current workload. They are reliable and maintain steady performance, ensuring they don't overextend themselves or compromise the quality of their work. This balanced approach helps them remain consistent and dependable, though it may limit their ability to seize opportunities that require greater flexibility or immediate action.

Tips to Become an A Performer:

- Pay attention to team needs and look for moments where you can step in and help.
- Take on one additional task each week, even if it requires stepping slightly outside your comfort zone.
- Learn to balance existing duties with new opportunities to avoid feeling overwhelmed.

C Performers: Avoiding Extra Responsibilities

C Performers often avoid taking on additional responsibilities, which others quickly notice. This reluctance can create the perception of disengagement or lack of initiative, limiting opportunities for growth and advancement. By focusing first on mastering their primary responsibilities, C Performers can build confidence and gradually begin to take on small, manageable additional tasks.

C Performers often face challenges stepping up to take on additional responsibilities due to a reluctance to move outside their comfort zones. This hesitancy can lead to a lack of initiative, as they may avoid volunteering for extra tasks even when opportunities arise. Over time, this behavior can create a perception of disengagement among colleagues and managers, further limiting their growth and potential for advancement.

Tips for C Performers to Move Up:

- Focus on excelling in your current responsibilities to build confidence.
- Volunteer for one manageable task to show initiative without feeling overwhelmed.
- Use small wins to gain momentum and take on slightly bigger responsibilities over time.

The Bottom Line

Taking on additional responsibilities demonstrates initiative, builds trust, and opens doors to greater opportunities. A Performers proactively seek

TAKE ON ADDITIONAL TASKS

out these tasks, B Performers step up selectively, and C Performers can begin by mastering the basics and gradually taking on more. Regardless of your starting point, small, consistent efforts to expand your responsibilities will enhance your skills, reputation, and opportunities for growth.

11

EDUCATION AND EXPERIENCE, THE FOUNDATION FOR LIFELONG SUCCESS

Education and experience are the twin pillars that support personal and professional growth. Some people rely heavily on formal education to pave the way, while others build their success through the hard lessons of experience. In reality, both are essential. Formal education provides the foundation for structured learning, while life experience refines and shapes our skills over time.

As leaders, it's important to embrace the pursuit of knowledge as a lifelong endeavor. Along the way, we must also remember an essential truth: Experience is often the best teacher. Let's explore how education and experience work together to influence our growth and how they shape our journey at different stages of life.

The Building Blocks: Traditional Education

The education journey begins early in life, laying the groundwork for intellectual, emotional, and social development.

Early Foundations
Learning starts long before formal schooling. Children absorb information from their surroundings, interactions, and experiences, even as infants. For example, my grandson Kent is only eight months old, but his time in daycare is already teaching him social skills that will serve as a foundation for more structured learning in preschool and beyond.

Elementary and High School
Children learn essential skills like math, reading, and problem-solving while navigating social dynamics in school. These years are critical for forming habits and attitudes that will carry into adulthood. Schools also help students develop critical thinking and collaboration skills, setting the stage for future success.

Higher Education and Beyond
For many, the path continues through college or technical training. I earned my degree in Building Construction from Georgia Tech, a milestone I'm proud of. The opportunities for one and two-year certificates at trade and technical schools provide great value and learning opportunities when a 4-6 year

major college investment and experience is not available or of interest. These programs equip individuals with specific skill sets that lead to long and successful careers. Finally, some people pursue higher levels of education, including a Master's Degree and even a Doctoral Degree, to satisfy their educational goals. This is not for everyone, but for some people, it adds value to their careers.

However, it's also important to note that success isn't limited to those with a degree. Some of the most accomplished individuals I know never attended college. Their classroom was the real world, where they gained expertise through perseverance, hard work, and creativity.

Life Lessons: Experience as an Educator

Once formal education ends, real learning begins. Life becomes the teacher, offering lessons shaping values, attitudes, and skills.

Licensing and Accreditation

Certifications and licenses are essential in many fields. Professions like real estate, plumbing, and healthcare rely on credentials demonstrating knowledge and commitment. These certifications open doors and signify a dedication to excellence.

Books, Podcasts, and Learning Resources

Leaders are lifelong learners. Reading books, listening to podcasts, or participating in online courses are all ways to gain new insights. You don't need to spend hours each day—small habits, like listening to an audiobook during your commute or dedicating 15 minutes to a professional journal, can significantly impact over time.

Networking Through Industry Associations

Joining industry associations provides access to seminars, workshops, and retreats. These forums expand your knowledge and connect you with like-minded professionals, fostering learning and collaboration.

Education and Experience in Action

The combination of education and experience is where true growth happens. Whether you hold a doctorate or never graduated high school, success ultimately depends on how you apply what you've learned. Performance is driven by attitude, motivation, and work ethic—education and experience are simply the tools that support your efforts.

A Performers: Lifelong Learners

A Performers are relentless in their pursuit of growth. They embrace opportunities to learn through traditional education and life experiences, understanding that every challenge is a chance to grow. Whether earning a degree, attending a workshop, or learning from a setback, A Performers actively seek knowledge and apply it effectively.

To maintain A-level performance, it's essential to stay curious and continually seek opportunities to expand your knowledge and skills. Experiment with different learning methods, such as reading books, taking courses, or engaging in hands-on experiences, to discover what resonates most with you. Most importantly, apply what you learn—turning knowledge into actionable steps ensures it has a meaningful impact on your personal and professional growth.

B Performers: Inconsistent Learners

B Performers value education and recognize its importance, but they often struggle to consistently pursue it fully. They may begin with enthusiasm and determination, diving into new learning opportunities, but this initial momentum frequently wanes. Competing priorities, time constraints, or a lack of clear direction can cause them to lose focus, resulting in incomplete efforts or abandoned goals. This sporadic approach not only limits their growth but can also create frustration, as they often have the potential to excel if they can maintain their commitment and follow through on their efforts.

Tips to Become an A Performer:

- Set aside weekly time for focused learning through reading, webinars, or podcasts.
- Even dedicating an hour a week can lead to significant growth over time.
- Share your learning goals with a mentor or colleague who can help you stay on track.

C Performers: Resistant Learners

C Performers often hesitate to pursue education or growth opportunities, citing a lack of time, interest, or confidence. This resistance keeps them stagnant and limits their ability to improve. However, even small steps can spark progress toward greater engagement and development.

Tips for C Performers to Move Up:

- Identify one skill or subject that interests you and commit to learning about it for 30 minutes weekly.
- Partner with someone who can encourage and hold you accountable for your growth.
- Acknowledge and reward progress to build momentum and confidence.

The Bottom Line

Education and experience are the foundation for personal and professional success. While knowledge is valuable, its true power lies in how well it is applied. By combining what you learn with the lessons life teaches, you can achieve remarkable growth and inspire those around you. Invest in yourself. Read that book, take that course, and embrace new challenges. The ultimate goal isn't just to acquire knowledge—it's to use it to lead, create, and make a difference. By leveraging the strengths of both education and experience, you can build a foundation for lifelong success that benefits yourself and the people and organizations you serve.

A PERFORMER EVALUATION

Rate yourself on a scale of 1 to 5 for each Performance Category listed on the opposite page. Be honest and objective in your assessment. Once you've completed the ratings, create a plan for improvement by focusing first on the area that needs the most attention. After addressing the top priority, move on to the next and take a few minutes to re-read the chapter to focus effectively for the best results. Revisit and adjust your plan after 60 days, then again after another 60 days. This consistent approach will help you achieve long-term progress.

Rating Scale:

1. Poor

2. Moderate

3. Satisfactory

4. Superior

5. Outstanding

Performance Categories:

1. Attitude   1   2   3   4   5

2. Wake-up Frame of Mind   1   2   3   4   5

3. Self Esteem   1   2   3   4   5

4. Healthy Relationships   1   2   3   4   5

5. Strong Communication Skills   1   2   3   4   5

6. Consistent Start to the Day   1   2   3   4   5

7. Strong Work Ethic   1   2   3   4   5

8. Problem Solving and Teamwork   1   2   3   4   5

9. Identifying Skill Sets   1   2   3   4   5

10. Taking Additional Tasks   1   2   3   4   5

11. Educational Pursuits   1   2   3   4   5

PART 2

A ENVIRONMENT

INTRODUCTION TO ENVIRONMENT

Every organization has the potential to move up the scale of excellence—from a "C" environment to a "B" and from a "B" to an "A." For a leader, one of the most significant accomplishments is shaping an "A" environment where excellence is not just a goal but the norm. This journey requires an intentional focus on seven foundational components: Vision, Leadership, Structure, Commitment, Discipline, Communication, and Relationships. Together, these elements form the blueprint for an environment that promotes success from the inside out.

It's also important to remember that while great leaders may set the tone for excellence, sustaining an "A" environment is a team effort. Leadership creates the vision, establishes the structure, and provides the tools, but the responsibility doesn't stop there. Every person in the organization, from the corner office to the front lines, plays a role in maintaining and improving the culture. When team members take ownership, engage in the mission, and contribute their ideas, the "A" environment moves from being a leader's goal to a shared reality. Excellence isn't achieved by a single individual—it's built and sustained by everyone working together, consistently investing in the vision, and holding each other accountable. When the entire team commits to this mindset, the organization doesn't just achieve excellence—it creates a legacy of an A Environment.

The principles of the A Environment are far-reaching inside all organizations. The high-level structure at the top is where to start laying the foundation. However, the seven components also relate to divisions, satellite offices, internal departments, sales teams, and affiliate companies. Each of these is its own environment, and the goal will be to consider how to implement the A Environment principles in each one. You may not be the CEO or President, but if you lead a division or manage a department of any size, embrace this material to have you and your team become the best you can be.

Working With Partners: A Two-Way Street

An A Environment inspires high performance in your internal team and among your close external partners—those vital associates who provide regular support and resources to help deliver your product or service to the marketplace. In industries like home-building, these partners might include suppliers, subcontractors, and service providers such as bankers and mortgage lenders. But no matter the field, every business relies on partnerships to function at its highest level. Manufacturing, professional services, and product-based companies need consistent, dependable collaboration from these external entities. The more we cultivate an "A" environment within our walls, the better equipped our partners are to offer top-notch support in return.

To foster an "A" environment, ensure your partners have the information, resources, and respect they need to deliver their best. When they feel like integral parts of the team, they're more likely to create "A" environments within their own operations, leading to better service and stronger results—a genuine win-win for all.

Embrace the Challenge: Overcoming Hurdles Together

Each of the seven components plays a critical role in creating this culture of excellence. As you move forward, consider how each can impact your organization's unique goals and challenges. Every company will prioritize differently, depending on specific needs and objectives. Begin by addressing the areas that require the most attention. Include your team and partners in this journey, welcoming their insights and suggestions, which will foster a sense of ownership and accountability. This level of engagement not only solidifies their commitment but also creates a support system, making each improvement sustainable.

The Bottom Line

In any change, there will be obstacles. Resistance is natural because, as the saying goes, "only babies like change." However, by focusing on the positive impacts for everyone involved, these challenges can be addressed, adjustments made, and a path cleared toward sustained growth. As you progress, move from one component to the next, continuously refining your environment. Remember, building and maintaining an "A" environment is not a one-time achievement but an ongoing commitment. With every improvement, you pave the way for sustained success, inspiring top performance in everyone from your core team to your trusted external partners.

A Environment Evaluation

An evaluation survey at the end of this book section will help you assess where you currently stand as an A, B, or C Environment. This will help you identify areas of growth and enhancement. Review this Evaluation Form and conduct a self-rating as you reach each chapter. Initially, pay special attention to the seven primary components of the A Environment; they are the driving force for the overall culture. Try to be honest with yourself. After all of the topics inside this book have been evaluated, pick one or two to focus on for the most impactful improvement. Don't attempt to take on too much at one time. Once noticeable

INTRODUCTION TO ENVIRONMENT

progress has been made, move on to the next one, two, and so on until all topics have been addressed and you've achieved A Environment status in all categories.

12

VISION – DEFINING PURPOSE AND DIRECTION

Without vision, leadership, and direction, you will end up somewhere, but you don't know where it will be, and you won't know when you get there. Let me explain.

Vision is the compass that guides an organization, pointing the way toward its ultimate goals. A clear vision ensures every team member and partner understands *where* the organization is heading and *why* it exists. Whether expressed as a mission statement, core values, or a concise description, vision serves as the foundation for every effort and decision within an organization.

Without vision, an organization may move in multiple directions but lack focus, cohesion, and measurable progress. Without a clear target, how can your team perform effectively, and how can success be assessed? A well-defined vision creates alignment, ensuring everyone moves toward shared goals. It empowers teams to work purposefully, provides a framework for decision-making, and offers a benchmark for evaluating progress.

Crafting a Vision That Resonates

Creating a meaningful vision begins with understanding the specific products, services, or values your organization provides. For example, in homebuilding, companies may focus on entry-level homes, custom builds, semi-custom options, or small commercial projects. Each focus requires a unique approach, resources, and customer base. While diversification may seem appealing, evaluating whether additional projects align with the primary vision or risk diluting it is vital.

This principle extends beyond homebuilding. Consider a law firm—choosing a specialization like family law, real estate, or personal injury can lay a strong foundation for success. In larger firms with multiple disciplines, setting a vision for each practice area keeps teams focused while reinforcing the organization's overarching mission. The key is to ensure that every initiative aligns with the central vision, creating unity and purpose across all levels of the organization.

Crafting Purposeful Statements

A strong vision statement should be clear, concise, and inspiring. It encapsulates the essence of your organization's purpose in a few sentences or focused bullet points, giving direction and motivation to your team.

VISION – DEFINING PURPOSE AND DIRECTION

Here are examples of impactful vision statements:

- "We aim to provide affordable, high-quality products efficiently, ensuring exceptional customer satisfaction."
- "Our mission is excellence in customer service, achieved through commitment to quality, clear communication, and effective issue resolution."
- "We will deliver the highest level of service in a welcoming environment, engaging our customers and earning their loyalty."
- "Our goal is eco-friendly production, supporting environmental sustainability valued by our customers and community."
- "We are dedicated to delivering quality homes by maintaining transparent pricing, smooth contract processes, and clear communication at every stage."

These statements go beyond being words on paper. They breathe life into an organization's purpose, becoming a rallying point for everyone involved. When teams connect with the vision, their work gains meaning and direction, fostering a culture of engagement and purpose.

Vision Across Departments and Divisions

Vision is not limited to the organization as a whole; it can and should be tailored to specific departments, divisions, or locations. A department-level vision reflects unique objectives while aligning with the broader organizational mission.

For example, an IT department might adopt a vision to "enable seamless technology solutions that empower teams and elevate customer experience." Similarly, a marketing team's vision could be "to inspire customers through creative storytelling and innovative campaigns that align with our brand's mission." These tailored statements ensure that every team's efforts contribute to the overarching vision, creating unity and focus across the organization.

Incorporating Vision into Everyday Operations

A vision is only as effective as its implementation. To create real impact, it must be shared openly, embraced by the team, and integrated into daily actions and decisions. Leaders play a critical role in keeping the vision front and center, consistently reinforcing its importance through communication, recognition, and accountability.

Encourage teams to internalize the vision by discussing it regularly, applying it to their roles, and using it as a guide for decision-making. When vision drives every action, it fuels sustainable growth, builds trusted partnerships, and fosters a culture of purpose.

A Performers: Champions of Vision

A Performers recognize the transformative power of vision and fully embrace it as a guiding force in their work. They align their actions with organizational goals, ensuring their efforts directly contribute to meaningful progress. Their commitment to the vision inspires their teams, creating a shared sense of purpose that drives collaboration and achievement. By consistently prioritizing the vision, A Performers help maintain focus and momentum within their organizations.

A Performers integrate the vision into their daily actions and decision-making processes to sustain A-level performance, ensuring every effort reflects the organization's purpose. They act as role models, consistently communicating the vision with clarity and enthusiasm while demonstrating its value through their behavior. Additionally, they regularly evaluate whether their team's efforts align with the broader organizational vision, making necessary adjustments to stay on course. This combination of living the vision, inspiring others, and fostering alignment ensures that A Performers remain catalysts for sustained success and growth.

B Performers: Steady but Cautious

B Performers recognize the importance of having a clear vision and understand how it can guide organizational success, but they often struggle to fully integrate it into their daily actions. While they are steady contributors who reliably complete tasks and fulfill their responsibilities, they may lack the initiative or confidence to align their efforts with the broader organizational goals. This can create a disconnect between their work and the overall vision, limiting their ability to make a meaningful impact. Often, B Performers benefit from encouragement and support from leaders or peers to help them see how their contributions fit into the bigger picture.

Tips to Become an A Performer:

- Ensure you fully understand the organization's vision and how your role supports it.
- Regularly reflect on how your tasks and responsibilities contribute to the overall mission.
- Look for opportunities to champion the vision within your team, even in small ways.

C Performers: Lacking Vision Alignment

C Performers often face significant challenges when understanding or connecting with the organization's vision. This lack of connection can result in a sense of disengagement as they struggle to see how their individual efforts contribute to the overall goals of the organization. Without a clear understanding of the vision, they may focus solely on completing tasks to finish them, without considering how these tasks fit into the bigger picture or drive progress toward shared objectives. This limited perspective not only reduces the impact of their work but can also create inefficiencies and missed opportunities for collaboration.

Tips for C Performers to Move Up:

- Take time to understand the organization's purpose and goals, and ask for clarification if needed.
- Identify one or two ways your work aligns with the vision and focus on improving your contribution in those areas.
- Work closely with others who clearly understand the vision to gain insight and inspiration.

The Bottom Line

A clear vision is the foundation of every successful organization. It provides direction, fosters alignment, and inspires purpose. When everyone understands where they're going and why, collaboration becomes more meaningful, decisions become more effective, and progress becomes measurable. Take time to define a vision that resonates. Share it openly, live it daily, and invite your team to embrace it. By doing so, you create a unified pathway to success, building an organization that achieves its goals and inspires everyone involved to contribute their best. That's the power of a vision lived out.

13

LEADERSHIP – THE CORNERSTONE OF AN A ENVIRONMENT

Defining a vision is the first step toward creating an "A" environment. Leadership is the driving force that turns potential into performance, guiding teams toward a shared purpose and measurable success. People naturally want to follow leaders who inspire confidence, build trust, and create clarity in uncertain times.

Effective leadership transcends age, industry, or background. It's not about authority—it's about influence and service. Great leaders consistently practice key principles that empower their teams and foster a culture of excellence. Let's explore the essential traits of impactful leadership and how they contribute to building and sustaining an "A" environment.

Key Traits of Effective Leadership

- **Providing a Healthy Vision**
A leader's role isn't just to define the vision but to communicate and champion it. An inspiring vision provides a purpose, aligning everyone's efforts toward shared goals. It motivates teams and partners to contribute meaningfully to long-term success. Leadership means painting a compelling picture of the future that people are excited to build together.
- **Defining Reality**
A leader's first responsibility is to face reality head-on. A clear-eyed assessment of the environment, resources, and challenges is crucial for sound decision-making. For example, a home builder must evaluate raw land availability, labor resources, and supply chain stability to ensure operations run smoothly. Ignoring these realities leads to missteps and unfavorable outcomes. Great leaders confront the truth, even when it's uncomfortable, and use that clarity to guide their teams effectively.
- **Motivating with Empathy and Compassion**
Emotionally intelligent leaders understand the importance of connecting with their teams. By showing genuine care, providing constructive feedback, and respecting individual differences, leaders inspire loyalty and engagement. A great leader recognizes that each person is motivated

differently and tailors their approach to foster commitment and productivity.

- **Being Approachable**
Approachability is a cornerstone of effective leadership. Leaders must be accessible, ensuring team members feel comfortable seeking guidance or sharing concerns. An open-door policy fosters trust, encourages collaboration, and empowers individuals to contribute their best ideas. When leaders are approachable, they create a supportive environment where communication thrives.

- **Delegating Effectively**
Delegation is not a sign of weakness—it's a mark of confidence in your team. Entrusting others with responsibilities allows leaders to focus on strategic priorities while developing their team's capabilities. Thoughtful delegation sends a powerful message: "I believe in your ability." As team members rise to the occasion, the organization becomes stronger and more cohesive.

- **Solving Problems Strategically**
Leaders must navigate challenges with a solution-focused mindset, turning obstacles into opportunities. Effective problem-solving isn't just about resolving issues; it's about teaching others to approach problems strategically. By modeling rational, proactive thinking, leaders empower their teams to handle future

challenges independently, reducing dependency and fostering resilience.

- **Practicing Patience**
Leaders often see the big picture before their teams do, but patience is essential in guiding others toward that vision. While maintaining momentum is important, leaders must give team members the time and space to absorb new ideas and contribute meaningfully. Patience builds trust, encourages collaboration, and creates an environment where innovation can thrive.

- **Recognizing and Developing Future Leaders**
Exceptional leaders identify and nurture talent within their teams. By empowering individuals to take on leadership roles, they strengthen the organization and ensure long-term success. Not everyone aspires to senior leadership, and that's okay—effective leaders respect diverse ambitions and provide opportunities for growth at all levels, valuing each person's unique contributions.

A Performers: Exemplars of Leadership

A Performers excel in leadership by setting the standard for others to follow. They lead by example, demonstrating the principles of effective leadership through their actions and decisions. These individuals align their goals with the organization's vision, consistently inspiring confidence and motivating their teams to deliver exceptional results. By fostering a culture of trust and accountability, A Performers create an environment where excellence becomes the norm and success is shared across the organization.

To maintain their high level of performance, A Performers must stay grounded in reality by continuously assessing the current environment and adapting strategies to meet new challenges. They inspire through action, modeling the behaviors and values they want to see in their teams. Additionally, A Performers understand the importance of fostering growth within their organizations. They dedicate time and effort to identifying and developing future leaders, ensuring long-term sustainability and success. By balancing vision with action and prioritizing mentorship, A Performers reinforce their legacy of impactful leadership.

B Performers: Solid Leaders with Room to Grow

B Performers exhibit dependable leadership skills and contribute positively to their teams and organizations. They are reliable and capable, often ensuring tasks are completed and goals are met. However, they may struggle with consistency in key leadership areas, such as strategic delegation, where they could better empower their teams, or motivational engagement, where they might inspire greater commitment and enthusiasm from their colleagues. While they have the foundation for effective leadership, B Performers often require guidance or encouragement to push beyond their comfort zones and take on more dynamic or challenging leadership roles.

Tips to Become an A Performer:

- Clearly articulate the vision and connect it to team members' roles.
- Build trust by assigning meaningful tasks to team members and supporting their efforts.
- Invest time in understanding what motivates your team and adapt your approach to inspire loyalty.

C Performers: Struggling to Lead

C Performers often face significant challenges when embracing key leadership responsibilities. They may shy away from critical tasks such as setting a clear and inspiring vision, addressing challenges head-on, or empowering their teams to take ownership of their roles. This avoidance can stem from a lack of confidence, hesitation to step into authority, or discomfort with making decisive actions. Such disengagement not only limits their own growth but also impacts their teams, creating a ripple effect of reduced motivation, inefficiency, and unclear direction. Without strong leadership to guide and inspire, team members may feel uncertain about their roles, leading to diminished morale and overall performance. C Performers must overcome this reluctance to lead by starting small, taking incremental steps to build confidence, and recognizing the importance of their role in fostering team cohesion and success.

Tips for C Performers to Move Up:

- Identify your leadership gaps and seek feedback to understand areas for improvement.
- Make an effort to be accessible and open to team members' questions or concerns.
- Begin by delegating one task or initiating one conversation that reinforces the vision. Build confidence through incremental progress.

The Bottom Line

Leadership is the foundation of any successful organization. It transforms vision into reality, aligns teams with purpose, and builds a culture of trust and excellence. By practicing key leadership traits—defining reality, communicating vision, motivating with empathy, and delegating effectively—you create an "A" environment where individuals and teams thrive. Whether leading a small team or an entire organization, your leadership sets the tone for success. Commit to growing as a leader, empowering your team, and fostering a shared purpose. As you do, you'll not only achieve your goals but inspire others to rise to their potential, creating a legacy of meaningful impact.

14

STRUCTURE – BUILDING THE FRAMEWORK FOR SUCCESS

With a clear vision and effective leadership in place, the next step in creating an "A" environment is establishing a strong organizational structure. A well-defined structure provides the foundation for efficiency, clarity, and collaboration, enabling team members to thrive and contribute meaningfully. Regardless of the size or stage of an organization, a robust framework of roles, responsibilities, and systems ensures that everyone knows their part and how they fit into the bigger picture.

While some individuals may excel in unstructured environments, most people perform at their best when there is clarity in their roles and expectations. A strong structure doesn't mean rigidity—it means creating a balance of flexibility and accountability, allowing teams to adapt while staying aligned with the organization's goals. Let's explore the essential components of building an effective structure and how it drives success, which are the key components of a strong culture.

Defining Roles and Responsibilities

The foundation of any effective structure lies in clearly defined roles and responsibilities. This starts with identifying the core functions of the organization—such as operations, sales, marketing, finance, and product development—and assigning these to specific departments or individuals.

In smaller organizations or startups, roles may be consolidated, with individuals handling multiple responsibilities. For example, a team member might oversee both marketing and customer service. As the organization grows, these roles become more specialized, evolving into clearly defined job titles. An organizational chart can help clarify responsibilities, showing team members where they fit and how they contribute to the overall mission.

For optimal performance, leaders should strive to align each team member's workload with their strengths, dedicating at least 80% of their time to tasks that align with their core competencies. This ensures that individuals can excel in their roles while using the remaining 20% for developmental or supportive tasks.

Implementing Effective Systems

An organization's structure isn't just about assigning roles—it's about creating the systems that support day-to-day operations. These systems ensure consistency, efficiency, and accountability across all functions.

- **Policies and Procedures:** Clear policies and protocols provide team members with guidelines for performing their tasks effectively. In industries like healthcare or manufacturing, these systems are vital for maintaining safety, efficiency, and quality. Whatever the field, consistent procedures foster reliability and accountability.
- **Production Systems:** For product-based organizations, production systems streamline the journey from raw materials to finished goods. Whether modeled on Henry Ford's assembly line or adapted for modern industries, these systems ensure that operations remain efficient and cost-effective.
- **Technology and Applications:** Digital tools are essential for today's businesses, improving communication and workflow. Software like Microsoft Office, project management tools, and industry-specific applications allow teams to collaborate effectively and manage their responsibilities efficiently.

Establishing Strong Communication Channels

Communication is the backbone of any effective structure. Teams need clear and consistent channels to share updates, solve problems, and stay aligned. From email and messaging apps to in-person meetings, communication systems should encourage collaboration and minimize misunderstandings.

Face-to-face interactions remain one of the most effective communication methods, building trust and fostering stronger connections. Organizations should prioritize a mix of digital and personal communication methods to ensure alignment across all levels.

Developing Marketing and Sales Strategies

A strong structure extends to how an organization attracts and serves its customers. Whether through digital campaigns, traditional advertising, or word-of-mouth marketing, strategies should align with the organization's capabilities and goals. Once marketing draws in customers, an efficient sales process ensures a seamless experience, converting leads into loyal clients.

Building Structure Together

Involving your team in shaping the organization's structure fosters a profound sense of ownership and accountability. When team members are invited to contribute their insights and ideas, they feel valued and empowered, which enhances their commitment to the organization's mission. This collaborative approach strengthens morale and encourages innovation, as those closest to the day-to-day operations often have valuable perspectives on improving efficiency and effectiveness. When associates see their input reflected in the organization's structure, they take greater pride in their roles.

A Performers: Masters of Structure

A Performers excel at recognizing the importance of structure and its role in driving organizational success. They actively work to align roles, responsibilities, and systems with the overarching goals of the organization, ensuring clarity and accountability at every level. By fostering an environment where everyone understands their place and purpose, A Performers create a foundation for sustained productivity and collaboration. Additionally, they have the ability to adapt structures to meet evolving needs, demonstrating flexibility and foresight in response to changes or challenges.

To maintain this high level of performance, A Performers should regularly evaluate the organization's structure to ensure it aligns with current objectives and supports growth. Encouraging collaboration by involving team members in refining roles and responsibilities fosters a stronger sense of engagement and ownership. Staying updated on technological advancements and tools that enhance efficiency and communication is also essential for maintaining a dynamic and effective structure. These practices allow A Performers to remain agile and proactive leaders in their organizations.

B Performers: Reliable but Inconsistent

B Performers recognize the value of structure and often contribute positively to its development and maintenance. They understand that clearly defined roles, responsibilities, and systems are essential for the success of any organization. In their focus areas, they perform reliably, ensuring that immediate tasks and responsibilities are handled effectively. Their appreciation for structure makes them valuable contributors, especially in maintaining team stability.

However, B Performers may struggle with consistency when fully implementing or maintaining structural elements over time. While they excel in managing their own responsibilities, they may have difficulty connecting their efforts to the broader organizational framework. This can result in a limited perspective, where their focus on day-to-day tasks prevents them from recognizing opportunities to enhance overall efficiency or address larger organizational needs.

Tips to Become an A Performer:

- Look beyond your role to understand how the entire structure functions and where improvements are needed.
- Collaborate with colleagues to identify gaps or inefficiencies in the current systems.
- Study effective structures within your industry and adapt relevant elements to your organization.

C Performers: Struggling with Structure

C Performers often resist structure, gravitating toward informal or unorganized approaches that can lead to confusion, inefficiency, and missed opportunities. This lack of defined roles and systems makes it difficult for their teams to find direction or stay motivated, resulting in decreased productivity and morale. Without a clear framework to guide actions and decisions, priorities may be overlooked, efforts can become scattered, and collaboration suffers. Over time, this resistance to structure limits individual growth and creates challenges for the entire organization as team members struggle to align their work with broader goals.

Tips for C Performers to Move Up:

- Begin by clarifying your own responsibilities and ensuring they align with organizational goals.
- Implement simple systems to manage tasks and improve efficiency, such as to-do lists or project management tools.
- Make an effort to clarify expectations and responsibilities with team members, fostering alignment and accountability.

The Bottom Line

A strong structure is the foundation of any successful organization. It provides clarity, fosters accountability, and creates the conditions for teams to thrive. By defining roles, implementing effective systems, and prioritizing communication, leaders can build an environment where productivity and collaboration flourish. Whether shaping a startup or refining an established organization, investing in structure ensures long-term success. Involve your team in the process, stay adaptable, and continuously refine your approach. With the right framework in place, your organization will be well-equipped to achieve its vision and create meaningful impact.

15

COMMITMENT: THE FOUNDATION OF SUCCESS

Creating an "A" environment doesn't stop at vision, leadership, and structure—it thrives on commitment. Commitment is the driving force that transforms plans into action and potential into results. It is the backbone of any successful organization, ensuring that systems, people, and processes are supported and developed over time. True commitment fosters consistency, accountability, and resilience, creating a culture where excellence is not just an aspiration but a daily reality.

Commitment must permeate every level of an organization. It's not a one-time effort but a continuous process that shapes how leaders, teams, and partners approach their roles and responsibilities. By fostering a culture of commitment, organizations can align their efforts with long-term goals and create a foundation for sustained success.

Commitment to Internal Associates

The foundation of any strong organization lies in its people. A commitment to internal associates means fostering a culture of trust, inclusion, and professional growth. When team members feel valued and supported, they are more likely to invest their skills and energy into achieving the organization's vision.

This commitment starts with open communication and active involvement in decision-making processes. Leaders should prioritize recognizing contributions, offering growth opportunities, and creating an environment where associates feel safe and empowered. By demonstrating care and respect, organizations can inspire loyalty, productivity, and alignment with shared goals.

Commitment to Policies and Procedures

Policies and procedures provide the framework for how work gets done. They guide behavior, streamline processes, and ensure consistency across the organization. However, for these guidelines to be effective, they require a commitment from everyone involved, particularly leaders who set the tone.

While new policies may face initial resistance, staying committed to them allows time for adjustment and implementation. Over time, these structures create clarity and efficiency, ensuring everyone operates with a shared understanding of expectations and objectives.

COMMITMENT: THE FOUNDATION OF SUCCESS

Commitment to Systems and Technology

In today's world, systems and technology are essential for maintaining efficiency and competitiveness. However, implementing these tools requires more than financial investment—it demands ongoing support, training, and integration into daily operations.

Commitment in this area involves ensuring that associates are equipped to use technology effectively and that systems are regularly updated to meet evolving needs. When properly supported, technology can enhance productivity, streamline workflows, and foster better communication across the organization.

Commitment to External Partners

External partners play a vital role in an organization's success. Whether they are suppliers, subcontractors, or service providers, these partnerships require clear communication, mutual respect, and a shared commitment to excellence.

By prioritizing strong relationships with external partners, organizations create a collaborative environment where everyone works toward common goals. This commitment strengthens the supply chain, improves the quality of products and services, and ultimately enhances the customer experience.

Commitment to Continuous Improvement

An "A" environment is dynamic, not static. It requires a commitment to continuous improvement, adapting to changing circumstances, and striving for higher excellence levels. This mindset ensures that the organization remains resilient, innovative, and forward-thinking.

Encourage team members to seek better ways to perform tasks, improve service quality, and enhance efficiency. Regularly evaluate policies, systems, and relationships to ensure they continue to serve the organization's mission effectively. By fostering a culture of improvement, organizations stay ahead of the curve and ready for new challenges.

Commitment to Customers

Ultimately, every commitment leads back to the most critical one—commitment to customers. Providing excellent customer service is the cornerstone of long-term success. This involves transparency, clear communication, and building trust throughout the customer journey.

Whether the relationship is brief or long-term, organizations that prioritize their customers' needs create lasting loyalty. By delivering exceptional experiences, organizations position themselves for continued growth and prosperity.

A Performers: Strengthening Commitment

A Performers excel at demonstrating commitment by consistently aligning their actions with organizational goals and setting a positive example for others. Their ability to inspire trust and model excellence creates a culture of accountability and motivation within their teams. By ensuring their associates have the tools, training, and support they need to succeed, A Performers reinforce trust and show their teams that they are reliable and invested in their success.

To maintain their high standards, A Performers lead by example, adhering to policies, using systems effectively, and embracing continuous improvement. Their actions set the tone for the entire organization, demonstrating that commitment begins at the top. Additionally, they prioritize cultivating strong external partnerships by engaging openly with stakeholders and fostering collaboration. These robust relationships not only enhance trust but also contribute to mutual growth and success, ensuring the organization remains resilient and aligned with its vision.

B Performers: Building Consistency

B Performers value commitment but may struggle with consistency. To enhance their performance, they should focus on connecting their efforts to broader organizational goals, maintaining steady follow-through, and deepening their engagement with team members and partners.

Tips to Become an A Performer:

- Regularly follow through on policies, systems, and responsibilities to maintain momentum.
- Evaluate your daily tasks and ensure they align with the organization's objectives.
- Strengthen relationships by showing initiative and reliability, whether collaborating with colleagues or supporting external partners.

C Performers: Taking the First Steps

C Performers often hesitate to demonstrate commitment, impacting their effectiveness and relationships. They can take meaningful steps toward improvement by starting small, focusing on reliability, and embracing a growth mindset.

Tips for C Performers to Move Up:

- Identify one specific area—such as adhering to a policy or improving a customer relationship—where you can demonstrate commitment. Small wins build confidence and trust.
- Concentrate on following through with promises and tasks, no matter how minor. Reliability

is the foundation for building credibility and accountability.
- View commitment as a path to personal and professional growth. Identify areas for improvement and take deliberate actions to strengthen your skills and contributions.

The Bottom Line

Commitment isn't just an action; it's a mindset that drives meaningful and lasting success. It transforms intentions into impactful results by fostering accountability, excellence, and resilience across every level of an organization. From supporting internal teams to building strong external partnerships, upholding policies, and embracing innovation, commitment ensures that every effort aligns with the organization's goals. By embedding this dedication into the culture, leaders create an environment where trust thrives, performance excels, and continuous improvement becomes second nature, positioning the organization for sustained growth and long-term success.

16

DISCIPLINE: THE BACKBONE OF EXCELLENCE

With commitments firmly established, the next essential focus area is discipline—the glue that holds an organization's commitments together and transforms goals into consistent, high-quality outcomes. Discipline provides the framework that aligns actions with intentions, fosters accountability, and ensures every team member contributes to the shared mission. It's not just about rules or routines—it's about setting expectations, honoring time commitments, and maintaining the performance standards that drive excellence.

Without discipline, even the most visionary plans risk falling apart. Let's explore the key areas where discipline differentiates mediocrity and excellence.

Work Hours: Setting the Foundation

Defining and maintaining work hours creates the reliability and structure organizations need to function effectively. While these hours vary by industry and role, they establish the rhythm for operations:

- **Homebuilding**: Office staff typically work 8:00 to 5:00, while field staff may start earlier to align with supplier and subcontractor schedules. Sales teams often work retail-like hours, including weekends, to meet customer demand.
- **Healthcare**: Hospitals operate on 24-hour schedules, with nurses and other staff working in defined shifts, such as 7:00 a.m. to 3:00 p.m. or 12-hour weekend-only shifts in some specialized units.
- **Restaurants**: From 24/7 establishments like Waffle House to more limited service models like Chick-fil-A, each business defines its hours to meet customer needs and operational goals. Lucias, our favorite Italian restaurant in Roswell, Georgia, has evening hours only Monday through Saturday.

In today's world of remote work and hybrid models, organizations must establish clear expectations for when employees are available, whether on-site or remote; consistency in work hours builds trust and ensures that both internal teams and external partners know when and how to engage effectively.

Timing Expectations and Deadlines

Deadlines are the guardrails that keep projects on track and ensure customer satisfaction. Whether you're managing a construction timeline, an airline schedule, or a production order, adhering to timing expectations is non-negotiable.

For example:

- In-home building, meeting deadlines for permits, construction phases, and home closings keep projects on budget and customers happy.
- In airlines, a delay in flight schedules can create ripple effects across airports and related services, such as baggage handling or in-flight catering.

Clear and realistic deadlines drive accountability, align efforts across departments, and create a culture of reliability. By honoring timing commitments, organizations build trust with their clients, partners, and employees.

Performance Expectations

Discipline also involves setting and meeting clear performance standards. Whether you're on an assembly line or part of a creative team, precision and consistency are key:

- Tasks on an **automobile production line** must follow a specific sequence, ensuring each phase supports the next. A single misstep can disrupt the entire operation.
- For **sales teams**, meeting targets requires consistency in outreach and follow-up.
- For **customer service**, adhering to response time standards ensures clients feel valued and supported.

When performance expectations are clear and attainable, teams can focus their efforts effectively, leading to higher-quality outcomes.

Proper Order and Workflow

A well-defined workflow is essential for maintaining order and avoiding chaos in any organization. Whether managing a manufacturing facility assembly line or executing a complex corporate project, tasks must follow an intentional sequence to ensure smooth operations. Effective workflows prevent bottlenecks and minimize errors, allowing teams to function cohesively and meet their objectives with greater precision and confidence.

By sequencing tasks correctly, organizations can reduce stress on team members, boost morale, and maximize overall efficiency. A disciplined approach to workflow ensures that each step contributes meaningfully to the organization's larger goals, creating a cohesive system that drives success. When workflows are clear and structured, teams can focus their energy on delivering high-quality results, fostering a culture of productivity and excellence.

A Performers: Sustaining Excellence

A Performers excel in discipline by mastering the art of refining systems, modeling accountability, and encouraging excellence across their teams. They continuously evaluate work hours, workflows, and deadlines, ensuring these elements align with and enhance the organization's evolving goals and needs. This proactive approach keeps operations streamlined and adaptable, positioning the team for consistent success.

A Performers also lead by example, demonstrating unwavering accountability in their commitments. Their disciplined actions inspire confidence and motivate others to emulate their dedication. Moreover, they prioritize team growth by providing constructive feedback and offering support that helps team members uphold high-performance standards.

B Performers: Steady Strivers

B Performers understand the importance of discipline but may struggle with consistency in applying it across their roles. They tend to excel in meeting deadlines and maintaining basic expectations, but might lack the structured approach needed to fully align with organizational goals. To move toward A-level performance, B Performers should focus on developing habits that reinforce discipline and establish greater reliability in their work.

Tips to Become an A Performer:

- Focus on following through with timing commitments and workflows to build reliability.
- Ensure you fully understand performance standards and align your efforts accordingly.
- Establish habits reinforcing discipline, such as prioritizing tasks and setting personal deadlines.

C Performers: Work-In-Progress

C Performers often face challenges in maintaining discipline, which can impact their ability to meet expectations and contribute effectively. They may feel overwhelmed by the structure and processes in place, leading to hesitation or avoidance. By starting small and focusing on achievable goals, C Performers can build momentum and develop the habits needed for greater success.

Tips for C Performers to Move Up:

- Focus on adhering to one specific aspect, such as meeting a deadline or maintaining set work hours.
- Work with a mentor or colleague to develop strategies for maintaining discipline in your role.
- Celebrate small wins to build confidence and motivation for greater consistency.

The Bottom Line

Discipline transforms potential into excellence. It's the foundation that keeps organizations aligned, productive, and accountable. From defining work hours to maintaining performance standards and streamlining workflows, discipline ensures everyone understands their role and delivers their best. By fostering a culture of discipline, leaders create an environment where commitments are honored, results are consistent, and excellence becomes the norm. This is the backbone of every successful "A" environment.

17

COMMUNICATION: THE LIFELINE OF AN A ENVIRONMENT

After establishing discipline, the next critical component in building a productive and effective workplace is communication. Communication in an organizational context goes beyond personal skills—it's about setting up clear, efficient methods that foster collaboration, minimize confusion, and keep all team members and external partners aligned.

Effective communication is the glue that holds the organization together. Without it, the vision, structure, and commitments can fall apart, leading to misunderstandings, disunity, and reduced productivity. Let's delve into the key communication methods and explore how to implement them for the best results.

Setting Communication Expectations and Goals

To communicate effectively, you need to be clear on the organization's goals and expectations for performance. This starts with sharing the organization's vision and objectives with every associate and external partner. When the team understands where the organization is going and their role in getting there, they can contribute more purposefully.

The first step is communicating the vision established in the earlier chapters, ensuring it's at the top of everyone's mind. Effective communication always starts at the top. As a leader, your role is to model clarity, consistency, and openness, setting an example for everyone in the organization.

Developing Communication Protocols

In today's workplace, communication methods vary widely, from emails to texting and from internal memos to virtual meetings. Each method has its strengths and appropriate uses. The key is to establish clear protocols for when and how to use each, providing clarity and reducing the risk of miscommunication.

- **Emails**: Email is the standard method of business communication. It allows for a documented, consistent way to exchange information and can be easily used for one-on-one or group communications. Email is particularly valuable for formal exchanges and situations where keeping a record of the conversation is essential. For professional service providers—like legal, financial, and insurance professionals—email is often required for communication, with legal standards requiring email records to be kept for several years.

- **Texting**: Texting is a convenient and quick way to communicate but is generally best suited for informal or immediate exchanges. It works well for short updates or urgent messages but may lack the formality and organization of email, especially in professional settings. Many organizations reserve texting for internal team use rather than official communications with clients or customers.

- **Internal Memos**: While less common today, internal memos can still be valuable for outlining policies, procedures, and essential protocols that need to be maintained as reference materials. When distributed as attachments in emails, memos are easily accessible and provide team members with clear, documented expectations.

- **In-Person Group Meetings**: One of the most effective methods of communication within an organization is regular group meetings. These meetings provide a space for team members to align on shared goals, discuss updates, and address pressing issues. To keep meetings productive, it's crucial to maintain a focused agenda and avoid letting tangential topics derail the conversation. Clear objectives, a set time frame, and a leader who stays on task can make these meetings an invaluable tool for coordination.

- **Virtual Group Meetings**: Virtual meetings provide many of the same benefits as in-person meetings but allow for geographical flexibility. With video conferencing tools, organizations can meet with team members, clients, or partners across different locations. Virtual meetings work well for project updates, strategy sessions, and brainstorming when in-person interaction isn't feasible. However, like in-person meetings, virtual meetings should follow a focused agenda to avoid wasting participants' time.

Utilizing Communication Tools and Applications

In many organizations, shared communication platforms streamline internal collaboration, creating more efficient and timely exchanges.

- **Shared Communication Software:** Tools like Slack enable real-time communication across departments, fostering collaboration and minimizing delays. This type of platform offers

instant messaging, project channels, and task tracking, making it easier for team members to stay updated and coordinate efforts.
- **Industry-Specific Applications**: For specialized industries, applications like BuildPro and SupplyPro (in construction) serve as centralized hubs where teams can access project-specific information. These systems reduce back-and-forth communication by providing a single platform for schedules, materials lists, and project updates, ensuring that all stakeholders have the information they need in real-time.

Building Relationships with External Partners

External partners play a vital role in supporting the organization's goals, and strong communication with them is crucial. Whether you work with suppliers, contractors, financial institutions, or service providers, clear communication fosters collaboration and helps partners deliver their best work. Your partners aren't mind readers, so the information you share—whether timelines, specifications, or updates—helps them meet expectations and ensures alignment across all stages of delivery.

Effective external communication can take many forms: scheduled update meetings, routine progress emails, or virtual check-ins for ongoing projects. By maintaining transparency and consistency, you build trust and create stronger, more productive relationships with your partners.

The Value of Personal, One-on-One Meetings

Among all communication methods, nothing replaces one-on-one, personal interaction. When possible, in-person conversations allow for deeper connections through eye contact, body language, and tone of voice. These cues make communication richer and more meaningful, ensuring that both parties fully understand each other.

Virtual one-on-one meetings are the next best option if in-person meetings aren't feasible. Video calls can replicate much of the face-to-face interaction, allowing team members and partners in different locations to have productive discussions that go beyond email or phone.

A Performers: Elevating Communication Excellence

A Performers excel in communication by recognizing their critical role in driving alignment, collaboration, and productivity. They consistently model best practices, ensuring clarity and meaningful dialogue in every interaction. By leveraging the appropriate tools—whether emails, meetings, or messaging platforms—they optimize communication methods to suit specific needs and audiences. Their ability to adapt their style to connect with diverse stakeholders inspires teams, strengthens relationships, and fosters a cohesive, high-performing environment.

A Performers also continuously refine communication channels, streamlining processes to maximize effectiveness and purpose. They lead by example, demonstrating professionalism, consistency, and clarity in all interactions, motivating others to elevate their communication standards. Additionally, A Performers prioritize building strong external relationships by offering timely updates, clear expectations, and constructive feedback.

B Performers: Reliable Communicators

B Performers understand the importance of communication but may struggle with consistency or adaptability. They often succeed in specific areas, such as team meetings or written correspondence, but miss opportunities to connect more deeply or use all tools effectively. To elevate their performance, B Performers should focus on sharpening their skills and broadening their communication approach.

Tips to Become an A Performer:

- Take initiative in communication by anticipating the needs of others and addressing them before issues arise.

- Develop fluency with additional communication tools like virtual meeting platforms or shared messaging systems.
- Regularly ask for input on your communication style from peers and leaders.

C Performers: Emerging Connectors

C Performers often face challenges in communication, whether due to unclear messaging, inconsistent follow-through, or underutilization of tools. This can lead to misunderstandings, inefficiencies, and strained relationships. To improve, C Performers should start small, focusing on foundational skills and building confidence over time.

Tips for C Performers To Move Up:

- Focus on one method of communication—such as email or one-on-one meetings—and commit to mastering it.
- Make it a habit to respond promptly to messages, follow up on tasks, and close communication loops. Reliability is key to improving overall effectiveness.
- Seek resources or mentorship to learn effective communication strategies, whether through workshops, webinars, or peer coaching.

The Bottom Line

In this chapter, we've explored multiple methods to establish clear, consistent communication in the workplace. Each method—from emails and memos to in-person and virtual meetings—plays an essential role in creating a well-functioning organization. To ensure your communication efforts are effective, make it a priority to monitor them regularly. If certain methods aren't working, adjust as needed. Effective communication is everyone's responsibility—from the CEO to entry-level associates—and helps ensure that every aspect of the operation runs smoothly. By creating a culture that values clear, timely, and respectful communication, you lay the foundation for long-term success and a strong, productive work environment.

18

DEVELOPING AND MAINTAINING HEALTHY PROFESSIONAL RELATIONSHIPS

In both life and business, relationships are the glue that holds everything together. They are the foundation of trust, collaboration, and growth. No matter where you work or what role you hold, relationships are critical to success. Even if you're a sole proprietor, your ability to interact with clients, partners, and suppliers will determine how far you can go. As I've said many times before, businesses aren't built on transactions—they're built on relationships. Strong professional relationships don't just happen; they must be intentionally developed and carefully maintained. If you can build bridges instead of walls, you'll find that success follows you wherever you go.

The Role of Leadership in Fostering Healthy Relationships

Leadership sets the tone for relationships within an organization. Owners, executives, and managers must create an environment where healthy, productive relationships can thrive. This isn't just about improving morale—it's about improving results.

When employees understand each other on a personal level, it's easier to work together professionally. When there's mutual respect and trust, teams collaborate more effectively, handle conflicts more gracefully, and produce better outcomes.

Leaders can encourage relationship-building through simple but meaningful actions:

- **Facilitate connections:** Host team lunches, celebrate birthdays, or hold informal social events.
- **Encourage collaboration:** Create opportunities for departments to work together on cross-functional projects.
- **Lead by example:** Build strong relationships with your colleagues and set the standard for others.

Internal and External Relationships

Professional relationships fall into two categories: **internal** (your relationships with coworkers) and

external (your relationships with clients, vendors, or other partners). Both are essential, but they require different approaches.

- **Internal Relationships:**
  Think of your coworkers as your "internal customers." These are the people you rely on daily to get work done, and they rely on you in return. Healthy internal relationships improve communication, reduce misunderstandings, and foster a sense of teamwork.
- **External Relationships:**
  External relationships often determine the success of your organization. Whether it's a key client, a supplier, or a trade partner, maintaining strong external relationships ensures smoother operations and builds goodwill for when challenges arise.

The Power of Long-Term Relationships

One of the most valuable lessons I've learned in my career is the importance of maintaining relationships over the long term. Over 36 years in the homebuilding industry, I've seen the same faces time and time again. Some of my strongest professional relationships have lasted decades; I can tell you firsthand that they've made all the difference.

A strong relationship isn't just useful during good times—it's invaluable during challenges. When issues arise, people who trust you are more likely to work with you toward a solution. That trust is built over time through consistency, integrity, and mutual respect.

What Happens When Relationships Don't Work?

Not every relationship will be smooth. There will be times when personalities clash, priorities differ, or trust erodes. In these situations, you have two options:

- Work to resolve the conflict and rebuild the relationship.
- If necessary, reassign responsibilities to minimize friction and maintain productivity.

For example, in my career, I've seen construction superintendents and trade partners struggle to work together. When it was clear the relationship wasn't salvageable, we reassigned roles to ensure the job got done without unnecessary tension. The key is to address these issues quickly, with professionalism and a focus on solutions.

Transactions vs. Relationships

Many businesses focus too heavily on transactions—getting the job done and moving on. While transactions are important, they're not sustainable without strong relationships to support them.

For example, homebuilding involves countless transactions: creating plans, sourcing materials, coordinating labor, and more. But when things don't go as planned—which happens routinely—the strength of the relationships behind those transactions determines whether the project succeeds or fails.

When you focus on relationships, the transactions will follow. Strong, healthy relationships lead to smoother operations, better results, and fewer headaches when challenges arise.

Three Tips for Building Strong Professional Relationships

- **Respond Promptly to Communication**
  Every relationship starts with trust, and trust is built on reliability. Return every phone call, email, or text in an appropriate timeframe. "Appropriate" will depend on the urgency of the situation—responding to a house fire is immediate, but responding to a new granite sample can wait. The key is to set expectations and consistently meet them.
- **Take Responsibility**
  When things go wrong, own it. Don't hide from mistakes or shift blame. Address issues head-on and do it quickly. Problems don't resolve themselves—they worsen with time. If you handle mistakes professionally and respectfully, you'll earn trust, even in challenging situations.

- **Be Professional and Polite**
    In high-pressure situations, emotions can run high. But no matter how frustrated you feel, maintain your professionalism. How you handle tough conversations will define your relationships for years to come.

A Performers: Building Bridges

A Performers excel at developing and maintaining professional relationships. They actively seek opportunities to connect with others, engage in meaningful conversations, and foster trust. They understand that relationships are built over time and require consistent effort.

Even in challenging situations, A Performers focus on preserving the relationship. They approach conflicts with a solution-oriented mindset and demonstrate respect for everyone involved.

B Performers: Relationship Keepers

B Performers excel at maintaining positive interactions and fulfilling expectations, but they often stop short of cultivating deeper connections that could drive greater collaboration and innovation. They are reliable and approachable, ensuring that relationships stay functional and cordial. However, when challenges arise, they may struggle to step out of their comfort zones and proactively engage in ways that build trust and strengthen bonds. To elevate their performance, B Performers should focus on being more intentional and proactive in their interactions, moving beyond the status quo to create meaningful, lasting partnerships.

Tips to Become an A Performer

- Proactively engage with colleagues and partners to strengthen connections.
- Be intentional about fostering relationships, even when it's not convenient.
- Prioritize open and honest communication to build trust.

C Performers: Task-Focused Builders

C Performers concentrate on completing their responsibilities efficiently but often overlook the relational aspect of their work. Their focus on transactions over connections can result in missed opportunities for collaboration and hinder long-term success. While they may excel at short-term results, this approach can damage their reputation over time if colleagues or partners perceive them as disengaged or unreliable. To grow, C Performers should shift their perspective from merely completing tasks to actively building trust and rapport. Developing stronger relationships—starting with a few key individuals—can help them gain confidence and demonstrate the value of investing in people alongside processes.

Tips for C Performers To Move Up:

- Shift your mindset from "tasks" to "people," recognizing the value of relationships in achieving long-term success.
- Focus on building trust with one or two key colleagues or partners.
- Commit to clear, consistent communication to improve reliability.

The Bottom Line

At the end of the day, professional success isn't just about the number of transactions you complete—it's about the quality of the relationships you build. Whether you're leading a team, collaborating with a partner, or working with a client, relationships are the foundation of everything. Create an environment that fosters healthy relationships, both internally and externally. When people trust and respect each other, they work better together, and the results speak for themselves. So ask yourself: Are you building bridges or walls? Are you someone people want to work with or someone they avoid? The choice is yours and starts with how you approach every interaction. Build trust. Foster respect. And watch your success grow.

19

PRODUCTIVITY DRIVES SUCCESS

As I've often said, organizations depend on transactions, and productivity is what powers those transactions. Productivity is the engine that keeps businesses moving forward, and its impact reaches every corner of an organization. Strong productivity means more efficient operations, happier employees, satisfied customers, and healthier profit margins.

But let's set the record straight: *being busy is not the same as being productive.* Many people confuse motion with progress. Moving papers, scrolling through emails, or extending conversations beyond what's necessary might make someone *look* busy, but it doesn't drive results. True productivity is about focusing on what matters most and executing with excellence.

The Productivity Mindset

Leaders have a responsibility to create an environment where productivity thrives. This requires clear goals, strong communication, and systems that support efficiency. Productivity doesn't happen by accident—it's the result of intentional effort and a culture that values results over activity. Let's explore the areas where high productivity makes the biggest impact:

Organizational Benefits of Productivity

Increased Efficiency

High productivity enables organizations to do more with less. It's not just about cutting costs—it's about maximizing resources to achieve greater outcomes. Efficiency is a cornerstone of success, and organizations prioritizing it often outperform their competitors.

Cost Savings

When productivity is high, costs naturally decrease. Teams use fewer resources, avoid waste, and complete tasks faster. However, cost-cutting has its limits—leaders must balance savings with maintaining quality. Cutting too deep can hurt morale, performance, and long-term success.

Improved Employee Morale

There's a direct link between productivity and morale. When employees feel productive, they experience a sense of accomplishment and purpose. A team that works efficiently and sees the fruits of its labor is more motivated to keep striving for excellence.

Enhanced Customer Satisfaction

High productivity leads to better products, faster service, and stronger customer loyalty. Whether you're building homes, running a retail store, or offering professional services, satisfied customers are the result of consistent, quality-driven productivity.

Strategic Goal Achievement

Every organization has goals—whether it's revenue targets, market share, or innovation benchmarks. Productivity is the vehicle that moves teams closer to those objectives. Without it, even the best strategies fall flat.

Productivity at the Individual Level

Organizations don't become productive on their own—individuals drive productivity. Leaders must equip their teams with the tools, time, and training to perform at their best. Here's how individuals can enhance their productivity:

Time Blocking

Allocate specific blocks of time for focused work. This minimizes distractions and ensures that important tasks get the attention they deserve. Leaders should encourage this practice by helping team members prioritize their time effectively.

Flexible Work Arrangements

The world has changed, and so have work habits. Remote work and flexible schedules have proven to boost productivity for many professionals. Employees can focus better and accomplish more by cutting down commute times and offering greater autonomy.

Goal Setting and Follow-Through

Clear, attainable goals are essential for productivity. Leaders must work with their teams to set realistic objectives, establish priorities, and provide regular feedback. Without goals, employees lack direction, and progress stalls.

Minimize Meetings

Poorly managed meetings are one of the biggest productivity killers. Meetings should have clear agendas, a defined leader, and actionable takeaways. Start on time, stay on topic, and end with clarity about the next steps.

Avoiding the "Busy" Trap

Busy work masquerades as productivity, but it's an illusion. Leaders must teach their teams to focus on meaningful tasks that align with organizational goals. This means avoiding distractions like unnecessary emails, social media, and unproductive conversations.

To combat the "busy" trap, focus on:

- **Prioritization:** What are the most important tasks today, this week, or this month?
- **Delegation:** Empower others to handle tasks that don't require your direct involvement.
- **Elimination:** Identify and eliminate low-value activities that waste time.

Building a Culture of Productivity

Creating a productive organization starts with leadership. Leaders must model the behaviors they want to see, set clear expectations, and celebrate successes. Productivity isn't just about working harder—it's about working smarter, with intention and purpose. Here's how leaders can foster a productivity-focused culture:

- **Communicate the Vision:** Help teams understand how their work contributes to the organization's goals.
- **Provide Resources:** Equip employees with the tools and training they need to succeed.
- **Encourage Feedback:** Create a culture where employees feel comfortable suggesting improvements to workflows and processes.

A Performers: Masters of Productivity

A Performers excel at productivity because they understand the importance of prioritizing what truly matters. They have a clear sense of purpose and align their efforts with the organization's goals, ensuring that every task they undertake contributes to meaningful outcomes. By managing their time effectively, A Performers avoid distractions and maintain focus on high-impact activities, consistently delivering work of exceptional quality. They don't just complete tasks—they approach each responsibility with a results-oriented mindset, driving outcomes that propel the organization forward. Their ability to balance efficiency with effectiveness sets them apart, as they meet deadlines and exceed expectations, inspiring those around them to strive for excellence.

B Performers: Steady but Reactive

B Performers are productive and dependable, fulfilling their responsibilities with competence, but they often lack the proactive mindset and strategic focus that define A Performers. They consistently meet expectations and complete their tasks, but they may struggle to identify and prioritize high-impact activities that drive long-term success. Without a clear emphasis on aligning their efforts with broader organizational goals, B Performers may focus more on completing immediate tasks rather than exploring ways to improve processes or take on additional responsibilities. While their work is reliable, they may miss opportunities to innovate or contribute to initiatives that could elevate their performance and influence within the organization.

Tips to Become an A Performer:

- Schedule focused work periods to improve efficiency.
- Ask leaders and peers how you can improve your impact.
- Challenge yourself to go beyond what's expected.

C Performers: Struggling with Focus

C Performers often confuse busyness with productivity, mistaking constant activity for meaningful contribution. They may complete tasks but struggle to deliver results that align with organizational goals or drive impactful outcomes. This lack of focus often leads to inefficiencies, missed opportunities, and a failure to prioritize what truly matters. Over time, this pattern affects their individual performance and can create frustration for colleagues and managers who rely on their contributions. Ultimately, this lack of clarity and direction can hurt their reputation, limit career growth, and undermine their potential to succeed.

Tips for C Performers to Move Up:

- Identify the habits or activities that waste time and replace them with purposeful actions.
- Focus on completing one high-priority task each day.
- Partner with a mentor or manager to track progress and stay on course.

The Bottom Line

Productivity is the heartbeat of every successful organization, driving innovation, powering transactions, and delivering value to employees and customers alike. It's not about doing more, but achieving more with purpose and focus. Leaders who foster a culture of productivity enable their teams to work smarter, prioritize what truly matters, and deliver exceptional results. Reflect on your own approach: Are you focused on meaningful tasks or caught up in busy work? Are you creating an environment where your team can thrive, and are you setting clear, actionable goals? Your answers to these questions shape not only your productivity but also your long-term success. By prioritizing what matters most and inspiring those around you, you can transform effort into meaningful achievements that propel your organization forward.

20

PROBLEM-SOLVING OPPORTUNITIES

This chapter connects directly to Chapter 8, where we focused on A Performer Problem-Solving at the individual level. Now, we're shifting gears to explore how these principles apply to teams. The dynamics change when a group tackles a challenge, but the opportunities for growth expand as well. In a team setting, every member has a chance to contribute, learn, and develop problem-solving skills—but only if the environment allows it.

That's where leadership comes in. Great leaders know they can't solve every problem on their own, nor should they try. Instead, they set the stage for collaborative problem-solving by creating an A Environment. This is where individuals feel empowered, supported, and motivated to step up, take ownership, and engage with the task at hand. The result? Not only do problems get solved, but teams grow stronger, more confident, and more capable over time.

This isn't just important—it's essential. At the organizational level, creating a problem-solving culture benefits everyone. It equips people with the skills they need to tackle challenges and ensures that problems are resolved effectively through collective effort. As a team member or leader, the question is, will you approach challenges with curiosity and a commitment to collaboration? If you do, you'll find that success often lies just beyond the next solved problem.

Identify the Problem

The first and most critical step in problem-solving is identifying the problem itself. Too often, teams rush into solutions without fully understanding what they're trying to fix. Leaders must resist this urge and guide their teams to ask the right questions:

- What is the problem?
- Why does it matter?
- Who is affected, and what's at stake?

Clarity is power. When you take the time to define the problem clearly, you set the foundation for meaningful solutions. And here's the key—problems aren't personal. They're not about blame or failure. They're puzzles waiting for your team's creativity and effort to solve. The better you define the puzzle, the better your team will put the pieces together.

Turning Problems Into Challenges and Challenges Into Opportunities

At the organizational level, reframing problems as challenges is transformative. Problems often feel like roadblocks, but challenges spark creativity and action. When a team shifts its mindset from "We have a problem" to "We have a challenge," it unlocks new possibilities for innovation and collaboration. This simple change in perspective profoundly impacts group dynamics, fostering long-term growth and stronger problem-solving capabilities.

Challenge, defined by Merriam-Webster, is "a stimulating task or problem."

The word *stimulating* is critical. A challenge excites the mind, motivating the team to engage and find a solution. In contrast, a problem framed as a dead end can create frustration, procrastination, or avoidance. The leader's role is to reframe problems as challenges that ignite curiosity and drive, setting the stage for meaningful progress.

Why Reframing Matters

Excitement and stimulation are powerful tools in problem-solving. When a team is energized by a challenge, focus sharpens, creativity flows, and results improve. Conversely, when interest and engagement are lacking, even the simplest issues can drag on unresolved. This is especially true when key stakeholders, such as decision-makers or resource controllers, aren't fully invested in finding a solution.

Effective leaders recognize that not every challenge will resonate equally with every stakeholder. They manage the situation by assigning tasks to the right individuals—those best equipped to engage with the issue. By aligning strengths with responsibilities, leaders can prevent procrastination or neglect while ensuring that challenges are addressed constructively.

Great leaders know that turning problems into challenges and opportunities is not just about resolving the issue at hand. It's about cultivating a team mindset that thrives on curiosity, collaboration, and continuous improvement. This shift is what drives lasting success, both for the team and the organization.

The Power of Turning Challenges Into Opportunities

Once a problem has been reframed as a challenge, the next step is to transform that challenge into an opportunity. This is where teams move from merely solving issues to seizing chances for growth and advancement.

Opportunity, defined by Merriam-Webster, is "a favorable juncture of circumstances" or "a good chance for advancement or progress."

At the organizational level, this transformation unlocks the potential for teams to assess situations more effectively and uncover paths for progress. Turning challenges into opportunities shifts the group's focus from obstacles to possibilities, creating a solution-oriented mindset. Teams that embrace this approach not only resolve their immediate issues but also strengthen their problem-solving skills, positioning themselves for long-term success.

Tips for Building a Solution-Oriented Team

- **Reframe the Issue**
  Help the team shift its mindset from "problem" to "challenge." This small but powerful change boosts motivation, opens minds, and encourages creative thinking.
- **Bring Solutions to the Table**
  Encourage team members to present potential solutions for group analysis. Create an environment where candid discussions are welcomed but remain respectful and constructive.
- **Leverage Strengths**
  Recognize the unique skills and talents of each team member. Delegate responsibilities

effectively by aligning tasks with the right people for optimal outcomes.
- **Communicate Clearly**
Clear communication is essential for success. Articulate the challenge, outline what's needed to solve it, and ensure everyone understands their role. Remember, clarity eliminates confusion and builds confidence.
- **Embrace Feedback**
Foster an open, positive environment where all voices are heard. New perspectives can spark innovative solutions; the best ideas often come from unexpected places.

A Professional Example of Turning Challenges Into Opportunities

In the early 2000s, JD Power and Associates—well-known for their consumer satisfaction surveys—expanded into the homebuilding industry. This shift caused concern for many companies, particularly high-volume builders with operations in multiple markets. For smaller, regional companies like ours, the news didn't just raise eyebrows—it became a defining moment.

At the time, we believed we were excelling. Our product offerings, productivity, sales, and profitability were all strong. Naturally, we assumed our customer service was equally exceptional. Then came the survey results. We ranked near the bottom of roughly 20 builders in the Atlanta market. It was a humbling realization—a true gut punch.

This wake-up call forced us to shift our focus inward. We implemented several targeted initiatives over the next few years to improve our processes and customer interactions. We didn't just address the issues; we turned them into opportunities for growth. By working together as a team, we climbed to near the top of the rankings within a couple of years.

The greatest reward wasn't the ranking, but the impact on our customers. They received better homes, improved communication, and an elevated overall experience. This transformation showed us the power of identifying problems, embracing them as challenges, and using them to create opportunities for lasting success.

The Mindset of a Problem Solver

Great leaders know that solving problems isn't just about fixing what's broken but how you approach the challenge. It's a mindset. They understand that yesterday's solutions won't always solve today's problems, and they stay curious, creative, and committed to growth. More importantly, they instill this mindset in their teams, fostering an environment where open minds and innovation thrive.

The best problem solvers don't simply address the issue at hand; they look beyond it. They turn problems into opportunities—chances to grow, improve, and create value. Every challenge becomes a stepping stone, and every solution adds another tool to their leadership toolbox.

If you want to lead effectively, you must embrace this mindset. Be open to new ideas, willing to step outside your comfort zone, and capable of encouraging others to do the same. When you lead with this approach, problems cease to be roadblocks. Instead, they become opportunities for your team to shine, grow stronger, and achieve greater success together.

A Performers: Opportunity Creators

A Performers excel at problem-solving because they see every challenge as a chance to innovate and improve. They approach issues with clarity, confidence, and a proactive mindset. A Performers don't wait for others to take the lead—they jump in, analyze the situation, and propose actionable solutions. They thrive in collaborative environments, leveraging team strengths and fostering creative dialogue for the best outcomes. Their ability to transform obstacles into opportunities inspires those around them and elevates the team as a whole.

B Performers: Solution Seekers

B Performers are reliable and capable, often finding practical solutions to problems. However, they tend to stay within their comfort zones, focusing on short-term fixes rather than exploring creative or strategic approaches. While they handle their responsibilities well, they sometimes hesitate to take the lead or involve others in collaborative problem-solving. B Performers have significant potential to grow into A Performers if they embrace a more proactive mindset and take steps to sharpen their skills.

Tips to Become an A Performer:

- Look beyond immediate tasks to anticipate potential challenges and opportunities.
- Collaborate more with teammates to gain diverse perspectives and spark innovation.
- Regularly ask for input on your problem-solving process to refine and expand your approach.

C Performers: Challenge Avoiders

C Performers often struggle with problem-solving, viewing obstacles as overwhelming rather than opportunities to grow. They may lack confidence, clarity, or the tools needed to address challenges effectively. As a result, they avoid engaging deeply with problems, which can lead to procrastination or unresolved issues. However, with the right guidance and support, C Performers can build the skills and mindset necessary to tackle challenges head-on and contribute meaningfully to team success.

Tips for C Performers to Move Up:

- Focus on solving one manageable problem at a time to build confidence and momentum.
- Seek clarity by asking for specific details about the problem and your role in solving it.
- Acknowledge small wins to reinforce a sense of achievement and motivation.

The Bottom Line

Problem-solving is more than just an individual skill or a group dynamic—it's a mindset that shapes how teams and organizations approach challenges. When teams tackle problems with curiosity, creativity, and courage, they unlock new possibilities for growth and innovation. Leaders who invest in developing their associates' problem-solving abilities create an environment where progress thrives, collaboration flourishes, and productivity soars. The world needs leaders who can inspire problem-solvers. Be the kind of leader who transforms obstacles into opportunities and challenges into victories. Keep your mind open, your attitude positive, and your focus steady on the goal. Leading with this mindset means no problem is insurmountable, and no group opportunity is beyond reach. Together, you and your team can achieve remarkable success.

21

GREAT CUSTOMER SERVICE STARTS FROM THE INSIDE

If you don't have strong internal customer service, how can you expect to deliver excellent external customer service? The reality is how well associates within an organization work together directly impacts the products and services delivered to the marketplace. Internal customer service is the invisible thread that ties all the moving parts together, ensuring everything runs smoothly and efficiently.

But here's the challenge: many organizations struggle with internal customer service. Even in the best-run companies, inefficiencies, communication gaps, and lack of coordination can derail the process. It's up to leadership to set the tone, define the processes, and ensure that internal service becomes a core priority.

The Three Pillars of Organizational Activity

Every organization, regardless of size or industry, operates on three foundational pillars:

1. **Operations** – Focuses on developing, manufacturing, and delivering the products or services.
2. **Marketing and Sales** – Promotes and sells the products or services to the marketplace.
3. **Finance and Accounting** – Manages the money and ensures financial sustainability.

Each pillar is vital, and their success depends on how well they interact. For example, operations cannot function without financial resources, and sales cannot thrive without marketing. These pillars must operate as a cohesive unit, like a relay race where one team member passes the baton seamlessly to the next.

In-home building, my primary industry, these three pillars often overlap and require precise coordination. From land acquisition to construction, from marketing campaigns to invoicing, every task must be synchronized to achieve the ultimate goal: delivering a high-quality home to a satisfied customer.

The Importance of Defining Processes

Processes are the backbone of internal customer service. Without clear, systematic methods, tasks fall through the cracks, deadlines are missed, and frustration builds. To succeed, every organization must define and refine its processes continuously.

Think of a relay race in track and field: each runner must know the leg of the race and execute it perfectly before passing the baton. In business, each department must complete its responsibilities thoroughly and on time so the next team can succeed.

Example: The Home-Start Process in Homebuilding

In homebuilding, the core task is simple: *put a house on a lot*. But to achieve this, several steps must align:

- Sales and construction agree on the house type and features.
- The drafting team produces architectural plans and a site plan.
- The designer creates the color selection sheets.
- The estimator calculates material requirements.
- Purchasing generates accurate purchase orders and budgets.
- Operations develop a detailed schedule and quality control checklists.

If any step in this process falters, the entire chain is affected. A lack of coordination between departments can delay the project, frustrate team members, and ultimately disappoint the customer.

Building Healthy Internal Customer Service

Developing strong internal customer service starts at the top. Leaders must create a culture where teamwork, communication, and mutual respect are non-negotiable. Here's how:

- **Create Awareness** Help associates understand how their work impacts others. Too often, employees are unaware of how their performance—or lack thereof—affects their colleagues. By fostering this awareness, you build accountability and encourage better coordination.
- **Promote Cross-Department Collaboration.** Encourage managers and department heads to work together to identify pain points and solutions. When leaders model collaboration, their teams are more likely to follow suit.
- **Provide Clear Communication** Internal customer service thrives on clarity. Define expectations, responsibilities, and timelines for each department. Ensure that every associate knows how their role fits into the bigger picture.
- **Address Issues Quickly.** When conflicts or inefficiencies arise, address them immediately. Prolonged issues can breed resentment and slow progress. Resolving problems quickly demonstrates a commitment to the team's success.

The Domino Effect of Poor Coordination

When internal service breaks down, the ripple effects are immediate and far-reaching. Sales delays can stall the drafting of plans and material estimates, inaccurate purchase orders can throw off budgets and disrupt construction timelines, and miscommunication between land development and construction teams can lead to site issues that derail entire projects. These inefficiencies go beyond logistical setbacks—they undermine morale, strain professional relationships, and chip away at overall productivity. When internal processes falter, the entire organization feels the impact, making it crucial to prioritize seamless internal service.

The Role of Leadership

Leaders are the architects of internal customer service, responsible for ensuring that every department operates as part of a well-oiled machine. This requires setting clear goals and priorities for internal coordination, fostering collaboration between departments to break down silos, and holding team members accountable for their roles in the process. When leaders prioritize internal service, they cultivate an environment where associates can thrive, communicate effectively, and work seamlessly together. This internal alignment enhances productivity and lays the foundation for exceptional external customer service, creating a ripple effect that benefits the entire organization.

A Performers: Champions of Internal Customer Service

A Performers excel in internal customer service because they understand the critical role it plays in driving organizational success. They proactively foster collaboration, maintain open lines of communication, and ensure their actions align with the broader goals of the organization. These high achievers not only complete their tasks efficiently but also anticipate the needs of their colleagues, ensuring that workflows remain seamless.

By modeling accountability and respect, A Performers set the standard for teamwork and coordination. They recognize that every interaction within the organization contributes to the company's overall success and consistently strive to strengthen these internal relationships. Their efforts create a ripple effect that enhances morale, boosts productivity, and ensures exceptional external customer service.

B Performers: Supportive Contributors

B Performers are dependable team members who generally excel at their specific responsibilities and contribute positively to internal customer service. They reliably complete tasks and maintain solid working relationships within their immediate sphere. However, they sometimes struggle to see the bigger picture, limiting their ability to collaborate effectively across departments or anticipate broader organizational needs. B Performers often focus on "doing their part" but miss opportunities to align their efforts with larger goals.

Tips to Become an A Performer:

- Take the initiative to communicate with colleagues in other departments.
- Engage with your team and leaders to identify areas where you can improve in supporting internal processes.
- Work on aligning your daily tasks with the organization's larger goals.

C Performers: Isolated Operators

C Performers tend to work within their silos, focusing narrowly on their immediate tasks without considering how their work impacts others. This lack of awareness can lead to inefficiencies, miscommunications, and missed opportunities to provide effective internal customer service. They often struggle with reliability and fail to engage in clear and timely communication, which can create frustration for colleagues who depend on their contributions. To grow, C Performers need to shift their focus from an individual task mindset to a broader view of their role within the organization.

Tips for C Performers to Move Up:

- Identify one colleague or department that depends on your work and focus on improving that connection.
- Commit to following through on tasks and meeting deadlines; even small improvements in reliability can build trust.
- Practice clear and timely communication. Share your progress and ask for clarification when needed.

The Bottom Line

Exceptional customer service starts with seamless internal coordination. When departments collaborate effectively, the benefits extend to employees, partners, and customers. Achieving this requires a clear vision that defines expectations for internal service, a culture of collaboration built on teamwork and mutual respect, and a commitment to thorough, well-sequenced processes. When associates understand how their work impacts others, they're more likely to take ownership of their responsibilities, fostering a positive cycle of accountability, efficiency, and success. Internal customer service goes beyond streamlining operations—it lays the groundwork for delivering an outstanding customer experience.

So ask yourself: Is your business a finely tuned machine, or are the gears grinding? The answer will determine whether your organization rises to greatness or settles for mediocrity.

22

MAXIMIZING IMPACT BY MASTERING YOUR FOUR KEY RESOURCES

Producing quality products and services requires using available resources effectively. Yet, all too often, leaders push their teams to do more with less, straining their capacity and jeopardizing results. To sustain success, you must learn to manage four critical resource categories: **Human Resources, Physical Resources, Money/Funding, and Time.**

Success isn't about having unlimited resources—it's about leveraging what you have wisely. Let's explore each category and how to manage them effectively.

Human Resources: Your Most Important Asset

Human resources are the heartbeat of every organization. Whether it's your internal associates or your close external partners, people drive the processes, innovation, and results that define your success. To effectively manage your human resources, you must focus on **balance**. Overloading your team with excessive demands or unrealistic deadlines creates chaos, burnout, and poor results. Instead, create an environment where people feel valued and supported.

How to Cultivate an Environment for People:

- **Show That You Care:** People don't care how much you know until they know how much you care. Invest time in understanding your associates' priorities and motivations. Treat them as people, not just "resources."
- **Provide Clear Direction:** Set performance goals and offer routine feedback. Periodic reviews should be meaningful, not just a checkbox exercise.
- **Build Loyalty with External Partners:** Treat your trade partners and suppliers with respect. If they know they can trust you, they'll prioritize your needs above others.

By managing your human resources effectively, you can enhance morale, loyalty, retention, and productivity. Conversely, excessive pressure and poor management can lead to unnecessary challenges and higher turnover.

Physical Resources: Tools of the Trade

Physical resources include the tangible items that allow your organization to operate—facilities, equipment, materials, and more. Without adequate physical resources, even the best-laid plans will fall apart. Questions to Consider:

- Do you have enough tools and equipment to meet your goals?
- Are you using resources effectively, or are inefficiencies holding you back?
- Are your external partners equipped to support your needs?

For example, in homebuilding, physical resources include land, machinery, building materials, and tools. These must be planned, procured, and deployed effectively to keep projects on track. Collaborate with external partners to ensure their resources are sufficient and their needs are respected.

If you consistently try to achieve more with fewer resources, your efforts will eventually collapse under the weight of inefficiency. Evaluate your resource needs regularly and plan ahead to avoid bottlenecks.

Money and Funding: Keeping Your Financial House in Order

Money is the fuel that powers your business. Without proper financial management, even the best teams and processes will struggle. Leaders must ensure that funding is available to support operations consistently. Financial best practices may include:

- **Plan for Stability:** Whether you rely on sales revenue or borrowed capital, ensure you have enough liquidity to cover payroll, inventory, and other operational expenses.
- **Pay Partners on Time:** Timely payments build trust and loyalty with external partners, ensuring they prioritize your needs.
- **Stretch Dollars Wisely:** Reducing costs is essential, but don't cut corners that affect quality or morale. Balance is key.

If financial resources are stretched too thin, productivity and morale will suffer. Regularly review your financial health with your accountant or banker to ensure you're on solid footing.

Time: The Great Equalizer

Time is the only resource distributed equally to everyone—24 hours a day, 7 days a week. The difference between success and failure often lies in how effectively you use it. Consider managing your time effectively by:

- **Prioritize Ruthlessly:** Focus on the tasks that deliver the most value. Use time-blocking to dedicate uninterrupted periods to high-priority work.
- **Eliminate Inefficiencies:** Avoid unnecessary meetings, reduce distractions, and streamline processes.
- **Respect External Partners' Time:** Show consideration for your suppliers and trade partners by minimizing disruptions and coordinating schedules effectively.

In homebuilding, a common inefficiency is the "dry run," where a trade partner arrives on-site only to find the job site unprepared. These missteps waste time and erode trust. Respecting your partners' time strengthens relationships and improves overall efficiency.

Bringing It All Together: Balancing the Four Resources

Managing resources effectively isn't about excelling in one area—it's about synchronizing all four. You might have plenty of money but lack the human resources to execute projects. Or you might have skilled workers but insufficient time to meet deadlines. The keys to continuously monitor and adjust are:

- Are we maximizing our human resources without overloading our team?
- Do we have the physical resources we need to operate efficiently?
- Is our financial house in order, with funding to sustain operations?
- Are we using time wisely to focus on what matters most?

Effective resource management begins with understanding project needs before diving in. Analyze the requirements for people, materials, money, and time to ensure each project is set up for success. Regularly monitor progress by checking in with your team and external partners to identify bottlenecks and make necessary adjustments. Equally important is listening to feedback from those on the front lines, as they often have the clearest insights into challenges and opportunities for improvement. By combining careful planning, consistent oversight, and open communication, you can optimize resources and achieve better outcomes.

A Performers: Resource Masters

A Performers excel at managing all four key resources—human, physical, financial, and time—with precision and purpose. They understand that each resource is interconnected and approach them with a strategic mindset. They prioritize their people, balancing workloads while fostering growth and morale. They ensure that physical resources are allocated efficiently, minimizing waste and maximizing output. Financially, they maintain stability, make smart investments, and avoid unnecessary risks. When it comes to time, they are ruthless prioritizers, eliminating inefficiencies and focusing on high-impact activities. They inspire confidence and trust, making them invaluable to any organization.

B Performers: Resource Managers

B Performers effectively handle most aspects of resource management but may lack consistency or struggle to see the bigger picture. They do a good job of maintaining the basics, such as meeting deadlines, adhering to budgets, and keeping projects moving forward. However, they may not always anticipate future needs or think strategically about how to optimize resources across all four categories. For example, they may focus on keeping costs low but neglect the morale of overworked employees or fail to communicate effectively with external partners about resource constraints.

Tips to Become an A Performer:

- Take a proactive approach to identifying and addressing potential resource gaps.

- Seek input from peers and leaders to refine strategies for better resource optimization.
- Focus on integrating the organization's larger vision into daily resource management.

C Performers: Resource Survivors

C Performers operate reactively, often focusing narrowly on immediate tasks without considering the broader implications of their actions. With human resources, C Performers often miss opportunities to build morale or foster collaboration, leading to strained relationships and higher turnover. Their handling of physical resources can be inefficient, causing delays or bottlenecks. Financially, they may either overspend to fix avoidable issues or underspend to the detriment of quality. They may struggle with prioritizing time, leading to missed deadlines or rushed work.

Tips for C Performers to Move Up:

- Start small by improving one specific area, such as better communication or meeting deadlines.
- Work with a mentor to develop a stronger understanding of resource priorities.
- Celebrate small wins to build momentum and gain confidence in resource management.

The Bottom Line

Your resources are the backbone of your business, and how you manage them determines your success. Missteps in handling human resources, physical assets, finances, or time can derail even the best-laid plans. But when resources are managed with wisdom and care, you create an environment where productivity flourishes, morale soars, and results follow naturally. As a leader, your responsibility is to maximize the potential of what's already at your disposal. Success isn't about abundance—it's about stewardship. When you manage your resources effectively, you empower your team to achieve extraordinary outcomes and elevate your organization to new heights.

23

INFLUENCE ON EXTERNAL PARTNERS

Do you fully understand how your environment affects your external partners—and how their environment impacts you? External partners aren't just vendors or service providers; they're vital collaborators who help drive your organization's success. From product suppliers to professional service providers, their contributions are integral to ensuring smooth operations and delivering high-quality results.

In homebuilding, these external partners include framers, electricians, landscapers, bankers, mortgage providers, and closing attorneys. For other industries, they could be accountants, IT providers, insurance agents, or legal counsel. Regardless of your field, your goal should always be to create an A Environment—a space where your external partners can excel in serving your organization. When you empower your partners to succeed, it creates a win-win situation that benefits everyone involved.

The Key to Success: Provide Clarity and Resources

The foundation of a strong relationship with external partners is clarity. They need accurate, timely information to deliver their best work. For example, a well-structured "start package" in homebuilding ensures subcontractors and suppliers have all the tools they need to complete a project efficiently. This includes:

- **Accurate architectural plans:** Poorly drawn plans lead to confusion and delays.
- **Detailed site plans:** Surveyor-provided layouts ensure proper placement and compliance with easements and setbacks.
- **Comprehensive purchase orders:** Clear and complete orders eliminate pricing and material errors.
- **Color selection sheets:** Properly documented interior and exterior design choices streamline execution.
- **Critical path schedules:** Sequencing tasks logically—e.g., framing before roofing—keeps the project on track.

When every component is well-prepared, your partners can perform their roles effectively, contributing to a seamless process. Remember, your partners are not mind readers. Your job is to provide the direction and tools they need to succeed.

Develop Mutually Beneficial Relationships

Strong external partnerships require more than just transactions—they need relationships built on trust, respect, and collaboration. While you may be the paying customer, treating your partners courteously and professionally encourages them to prioritize your needs.

Think about this: When your external partners schedule their day, don't you want to be their top priority? Create conditions that make your business the account they want to service first. Factors like well-maintained job sites, clear communication, and prompt issue resolution can make all the difference.

For instance, in my experience as a home builder, subdivisions that operated smoothly—with ready job sites and responsive teams—were always preferred by trade partners. Those that didn't operate efficiently? They were avoided. Strive to be the kind of client partners look forward to working with, and they'll consistently deliver their best for you.

Make Them Part of the Team

Inclusion is another critical factor in building strong partnerships. Your external partners are experts in their fields, and tapping into their knowledge can improve your processes and outcomes. Bring them into your strategy sessions or involve them in key decisions to foster accountability and ownership. For example, I often consulted with trade partners on plan designs and operational strategies. Their feedback helped refine processes, avoid pitfalls, and ensure better results. Additionally, these collaborations provided valuable insights into their decision-making and workflows, which I could adapt to improve my own operations.

Pay Them on Time, Every Time

One of the simplest yet most impactful ways to strengthen relationships with external partners is to honor payment agreements. Whether payments are due weekly, monthly, or quarterly, meeting these deadlines shows respect and reliability. Partners who trust that you'll fulfill your obligations are more likely to prioritize your needs and go the extra mile for your business.

A Performers: Leaders in External Collaboration

A Performers excel because they recognize that their success is deeply tied to the success of their external partners. They approach partnerships with intentionality, going beyond transactional interactions to build meaningful, collaborative relationships. By offering clear direction, fostering inclusion, and maintaining accountability, A Performers create an A Environment where their partners can thrive and deliver their best work.

Clarity is the foundation of their approach, as A Performers ensure that external partners receive detailed instructions and the tools they need to succeed. They actively involve partners in strategy discussions, valuing their expertise and promoting a sense of ownership. Above all, they honor commitments, from timely payments to transparent communication, reinforcing trust and loyalty. This ability to lead by example not only elevates the performance of external partners but also creates a ripple effect of excellence that enhances the entire organization.

B Performers: Collaborative Connectors

B Performers understand the importance of external partnerships and often maintain functional, positive relationships. However, they tend to approach these interactions with a task-oriented mindset, focusing on completing transactions rather than fostering deeper collaboration. While they communicate adequately, they may fail to anticipate partner needs or address potential issues proactively. B Performers generally honor their commitments but might overlook opportunities to strengthen trust or show appreciation.

Tips to Become an A Performer:

- Share updates and expectations in advance to avoid confusion. Clear communication sets the stage for success.

- Recognize and appreciate the contributions of external partners. A simple thank-you can build lasting goodwill.
- Follow through on promises and payment agreements to show reliability and earn trust.

C Performers: Transactional Operators

C Performers view external partnerships primarily as business transactions, often missing the relational and strategic aspects that drive long-term success. They may neglect to provide clear instructions, fail to meet deadlines, or delay payments, creating frustration and inefficiency for their partners. This approach can lead to strained relationships and a lack of trust, making securing their partners' best efforts harder. They can improve by shifting their focus to building trust through consistent reliability, clarifying expectations, and seeking feedback. They can transform strained partnerships into collaborative, productive relationships by prioritizing communication and dependability.

Tips for C Performers to Move Up

- Provide clear instructions and timelines to partners to prevent misunderstandings.
- Consistently meet deadlines and payment terms to rebuild trust.

INFLUENCE ON EXTERNAL PARTNERS

- Ask external partners how you can better support their work. Listening demonstrates a commitment to improvement.

The Bottom Line

Your external partners are not just service providers but an extension of your team. Treat them as such; they will reward you with loyalty, efficiency, and exceptional service. Creating an Environment for your partners benefits everyone. When you empower them with clear communication, timely payments, and inclusive collaboration, they can perform at their best, helping your organization succeed. Remember: success is a two-way street. The more you invest in your partners, the more they'll invest in you, creating a cycle of mutual growth and excellence.

A ENVIRONMENT EVALUATION

Rate yourself on a scale of 1 to 5 for each Environment Category listed on the opposite page. Be honest and objective in your assessment. Once you've completed the ratings, create a plan for improvement by focusing first on the area that needs the most attention. After addressing the top priority, move on to the next and take a few minutes to re-read the chapter to focus effectively for the best results. Revisit and adjust your plan after 60 days, then again after another 60 days. This consistent approach will help you achieve long-term progress.

Rating Scale:

1. Poor

2. Moderate

3. Satisfactory

4. Superior

5. Outstanding

Performance Categories:

1. <u>Vision</u>　　1　2　3　4　5

2. <u>Leadership</u>　　1　2　3　4　5

3. <u>Structure</u>　　1　2　3　4　5

4. <u>Commitment</u>　　1　2　3　4　5

5. <u>Discipline</u>　　1　2　3　4　5

6. <u>Communication</u>　　1　2　3　4　5

7. <u>Relationships</u>　　1　2　3　4　5

8. <u>Productivity</u>　　1　2　3　4　5

9. <u>Problem Solving</u>　　1　2　3　4　5

10. <u>Internal Customer Service</u>　　1　2　3　4　5

11. <u>Managing Resources</u>　　1　2　3　4　5

12. <u>Influence on External Partners</u>　　1　2　3　4　5

CONCLUSION

Your attitude is the foundation of your performance. From the very first chapter, we've explored how the mindset you bring to your day shapes the results you achieve. Whether you see yourself as an A, B, or C performer, one thing is clear: transformation starts from within. By understanding where you currently stand and committing to intentional improvement, you can unlock new levels of growth and success.

The journey to improvement begins with small but powerful steps. Starting each day with positivity, mastering your emotions, and celebrating even the smallest victories can create a ripple effect in your personal and professional life. As you address the factors holding you back and turn challenges into opportunities, you'll notice gradual shifts in how you perform, connect, and achieve. Progress is not about overnight success; it's about consistent effort, building momentum one step at a time.

As you move forward, focus on turning negatives into positives and leveraging self-awareness to guide your growth. With each deliberate action, you'll discover the power of aligning your mindset with your goals. Over time, you'll notice not only improvement in your performance but also a deeper sense of fulfillment and purpose.

PERFORMER ENVIRONMENT

Remember, this is a process—a journey of becoming the best version of yourself. Growth requires patience, persistence, and a willingness to embrace the lessons along the way. You have the tools, the insights, and the potential. Now, it's time to act. Embrace the journey, trust the process, and watch as each small improvement propels you toward greater success.

So, as you close this book, ask yourself: What's the next step you can take today to move closer to the life you envision? Whatever it is, take it. Start small. Be consistent. And watch how far you can go!

ABOUT THE AUTHOR

Farrell is a lifelong Georgian; he grew up in Savannah and moved to Atlanta in 1982. The relationship with his wife, life partner, and best friend, Kathy, started in high school in early 1981. They married in 1986, and have two daughters, Pfeiffer and Collier, who also live in the Atlanta area.

Farrell started his long awaited second career as a teacher, coach, mentor, and speaker in 2022. The Bell Curve of Life is his unique program that focuses on circumstances that people find themselves in on a routine basis, he is in the people business and the program is about personal and professional growth.

He is a former business owner and 36-year veteran of the residential land development and homebuilding industry. Upon graduation from Georgia Tech with Honors in 1986, he immediately entered the field in the Atlanta metropolitan area. His first management experience came at the age of 22, and for most of his career he held senior level positions with both privately owned and publicly traded companies.

Farrell can be reached through his website –
www.thebellcurveoflife.com